Instant Vegas®
Movie Studio™ + DVD

Douglas Spotted Eagle & John Rofrano

CMP**Books**

San Francisco, CA

Published by CMP Books
an imprint of CMP Media LLC
600 Harrison Street, 6th Floor, San Francisco, CA 94107 USA
Tel: 415-947-6615; Fax: 415-947-6015
www.cmpbooks.com
email: books@cmp.com

Vegas® is a registered trademark of Sony Pictures Digital Inc. or its affiliates in the United States and other countries. Throughout this book Movie Studio refers to Sony® Screenblast® Movie Studio™. Designations used by companies to distinguish their products are often claimed as trademarks. In all instances where CMP is aware of a trademark claim, the product name appears in initial capital letters, in all capital letters, or in accordance with the vendor's capitalization preference. Readers should contact the appropriate companies for more complete information on trademarks and trademark registrations. All trademarks and registered trademarks in this book are the property of their respective holders.

The programs in this book are presented for instructional value. The programs have been carefully tested, but are not guaranteed for any particular purpose. The publisher does not offer any warranties and does not guarantee the accuracy, adequacy, or completeness of any information herein and is not responsible for any errors or omissions. The publisher assumes no liability for damages resulting from the use of the information in this book or for any infringement of the intellectual property rights of third parties that would result from the use of this information.

Distributed in the U.S. by:
Publishers Group West
1700 Fourth Street
Berkeley, CA 94710
1-800-788-3123

Distributed in Canada by:
Jaguar Book Group
100 Armstrong Avenue
Georgetown, Ontario M6K 3E7 Canada
905-877-4483

For individual orders and for information on special discounts for quantity orders, please contact:
CMP Books Distribution Center, 6600 Silacci Way, Gilroy, CA 95020
email: cmp@rushorder.com; Web: www.cmpbooks.com

ISBN: 1-57820-271-X

Dedication

We would like to thank our families and the members of the various web communities for all their support and encouragement as we've written these books on Sony software products. Were it not for their questions and suggestions, this would be a much different book.

John would like to dedicate this book to his wife, Terry.

Douglas dedicates this book to his fans and friends.

Contents

Introduction

Welcome to the Suite World of Multimedia Creation

Sony Vegas® Movie Studio® + DVD, ACID® Music Studio, and Sound Forge® Audio Studio are a great suite of tools that will help you master the art of multimedia. These tools are the entry level tools in the Sony software family, but don't think for a moment that these tools aren't capable of producing top end quality. The output quality of these tools is the same as what you'll find in the full-blown professional applications.

In this book, John Rofrano will guide you through the technical and creative aspects of ACID Music Studio, enabling you to create wonderful royalty-free soundtracks in virtually every genre of music that you can imagine. Just think, you can create soundtracks for your family movies, school projects, and even corporate presentations, all within the ACID application.

Douglas Spotted Eagle shows you the ins and outs of Vegas Movie Studio + DVD, which will show you how to capture, edit, and burn your movies to a DVD so that you can share them with others.

Don't worry if you're a newcomer to multimedia. We start with simple language, and make the subject very user friendly.

This book is written for the newcomer, but you'll also find a lot of tips and tricks to help you not just learn the application, but understand more about the multimedia world than you'd probably anticipated.

So grab your camera and computer, and get ready to make your first movie!

This book is designed to raise your knowledge and skill level with Sony Vegas Movie Studio + DVD and Sony ACID Music Studio. On the VASST website, you'll find a downloadable zip folder that will provide you with the projects you see in this book. Visit www.vasst.com to download this folder of projects and media.

You may also find www.acidplanet.com a valuable resource from which to download hundreds of free ACID loops for your musical creativity.

Multimedia is more than showing video or making music. It's an art form, a means of expressing an idea, a concept, emotion, or message. Creating multimedia allows us to span cultural and social gaps, and send powerful messages disassociated from the authors. It provides an outlet for entertainment and information, creative expression and social involvement. Multimedia is becoming a powerful part of our daily lives, and knowing how to create, manipulate, and deliver it will soon be a component of many employment descriptions, much like Powerpoint has become in recent years. This book arms you with the tools and skills you can master in order to better comprehend and create.

Remember, Steven Spielberg started small too.

Douglas Spotted Eagle

John Rofrano

Chapter 1

Media Basics

In the multimedia world, there are lots of file formats that are used by an ever-broadening number of editing, authoring, and playback applications. Most of these formats follow some standards that allow a number of applications, but nothing is available that will open every format. Sometimes, this can be frustrating as the average user tries to work with formats not destined for editing, such as the DivX or Xvid formats. Even MPEG was not designed for editing in lower bitrates, but many users want to edit lower grade media for family home video, school projects, and even corporate work. Keep in mind that video downloaded from the internet is usually safe for personal use, but most often violates copyright laws, so you'll not want to be using it in your corporate work or video for resale.

Sony Vegas Movie Studio is capable of opening nearly any media type that you might have available on your PC, with the exception of a few streaming formats that are protected for copyright reasons. There are some "codecs" such as the M-JPEG codec that many still cameras use for video, that you'll need to download and install so that Vegas Movie Studio can read them. This "format-agnostic" benefit of Vegas Movie Studio means you'll be able to edit, insert, and deliver media without compatibility concerns. Notice all the media formats available in this shot of the Vegas Movie Studio Explorer window.

The most common file type used in Vegas Movie Studio and other PC-based nonlinear editor systems (NLEs) is the AVI file type, which is what Vegas Movie Studio creates when you capture video from your DV (digital video) camera. DV cameras are the most common type of camera in the world today. DV provides superior video quality and can be found in very small camera packages. There are a few things you should know about shooting DV, and we'll outline them in this next section.

Identification...	13.14KB	VF File
Keyframed Text	22.45KB	VF File
LowerThird	12.81KB	VF File
Matte#1	738.77KB	PNG Image
Model	172.86KB	JPEG Image
Model#2	264.49KB	JPEG Image
Pixelated Ima...	11.27KB	VF File
SinglePass Color	8.77KB	VF File
TrickyText	11.35KB	VF File
VegasMovieS...	502.83KB	Windows Media...
VegasMovieS...	484.08KB	Windows Media...
VegasMovieS...	490.33KB	Windows Media...
VegasMovieS...	321.56KB	Windows Media...

Through this book, we'll be referring to a number of different formats for editing and delivery. The most common format we'll be working with is the AVI format. This is what Windows uses for most video editing, and it is common across most NLE systems. However, there are other types of media formats that Vegas Movie Studio can work with on the Timeline, such as QuickTime and Windows Media Audio and Video. Additionally, Vegas Movie Studio can import all sorts of still image formats such as JPG, TIF, TGA, PNG, BMP, and others. For best results, work with images that are in TGA or PNG format. These are commonly referred to as "Targa" and "Ping" format files.

Shooting DV requires a little bit of production knowledge. Lighting and audio are important if you're after the best production value. Spending a little time on pre-production (before you start shooting) will save you a lot of time in the post-production stage (after you shoot).

For instance, the way the DV camera works is that it bases its color information on the amount of light that it receives. Therefore, the more light you have, the more color-rich your movie will be. You don't need big Hollywood-type lights to make a great video. Just be sure that if you're indoors that you remember to white-balance your camera and also be sure that you get as much light on the subject being videographed as possible.

You can use existing lights in your home instead of using professional lights, but be cautious and safe. Halogen work lights designed for construction work are not good alternatives, and they can start fires, explode, or burn people. Use safe lighting when creating your video masterpieces. There are many lighting books available that show the use of safe equipment or how to get good lighting from budget-conscious, safe gear.

Generally, you'll need at least one "key" or primary light, and some sort of reflective device such as the Photoflex popout reflectors.

Audio should be at the top of your priority list of concerns for creating a good video presentation. Sound is 70 percent of what your audience "sees" in the picture. Good sound will keep your audience focused and is critical to conveying the message that your video contains.

Look into purchasing a good microphone, or if the budget isn't available, simply remember that a cheap microphone close to the subject is infinitely preferable to a good microphone farther away from the subject. Here you see an Audio Technica ATR-55. This is a great budget or starter mic. Whenever possible, avoid using the microphone built into your camera.

A good tripod is very helpful. There is a wide variety of tripod and headsets available; buy what you can afford. Shooting with a tripod will tremendously improve video quality simply for the stability it offers.

If you don't plan on doing a lot of panning or tilting, you won't need a good tripod head, but if following fast action is important to you, you'll want a reasonably good tripod and head setup. Inexpensive tripods have the camera mount and head assembly built into the system, while higher quality systems have a separate head and leg assembly. This allows you to purchase low-cost legs (sticks) and a higher-cost and higher-quality head, so you can upgrade later as budget allows or shooting situations necessitate.

As you work with your camera, you'll want to spend a little time learning about picture composition, how to frame your subject in the viewfinder, and how to keep the image compelling. In the image to the left, notice how the image is framed correctly in the lower frame. In the upper frame, the subject is not framed correctly. Generally the image is divided so that the subject is never seen in the exact center portions of the frame, but rather seen to one side or another, looking across the frame at its widest point. So, if the subject is on the left side of the frame, they should generally be looking to the right, and vice-versa.

Chapter 2

Getting Set Up with Vegas Movie Studio

Vegas Movie Studio has minimum hardware requirements. Though you may be able to get by with less, it's not recommended. Here are the details to get you up and running fast with minimum fuss or muss. Even though you've likely already installed Vegas Movie Studio, here are some pointers in getting your computer optimized for video editing.

The Computer System

Vegas Movie Studio does not require any special or difficult-to-obtain hardware to operate. You just need to invest in a reasonably fast computer system, but not expensive add-ons (unlike some other NLEs). According to Sony, Vegas Movie Studio requires that your system meets the following minimum specifications.

- Microsoft® Windows® 2000, XP Home, or XP Professional

- 500MHz processor

- 150MB hard-disk space for program installation

- 128MB RAM

- OHCI compatible i.LINK® connector*/IEEE-1394DV card (for DV capture and print-to-tape)

- Windows-compatible soundcard

- CD-ROM drive (for installation from a CD only)

- Supported CD-Recordable drive (for CD burning only)

- Supported DVD-r/-rw/+r/+rw drive (for DVD burning only)

- DirectX 8.0 or higher (included on Vegas Movie Studio disk)

Note the word minimum above. You'll have a much better editing experience with a faster, more robust computer system.

Edits, FX, and filters will be faster to preview on a faster system.

Get more RAM. 1GB (one gigabyte) is suggested as the optimum amount for Vegas Movie Studio. You'll generally experience smoother playback from the Timeline and the ability to apply more effects (audio and video) without glitching. Vegas Movie Studio doesn't require any special hardware to run, so additional RAM gives it some of its magic.

Multiple hard drives might be something you'd prefer working with if you are serious about your videos. Working with video requires a lot of drive space. One hour of DV eats up about 13GB of drive space. It's best to put your Windows system on one drive with all the attendant applications, and store your video on a second drive. Beware of the partitioned D drives many computer manufacturers use. It's really just a split of the C drive, not a true independent drive. Make sure these other drives are 7200RPM with 8MB or more of cache for the best results. It's a good idea to format your drives as NTFS (not Fat 32) to overcome file-size limitations imposed by other drive formatting types.

You can use FireWire and USB external drives, too. We've had great success working with both iterations for general editing tasks. However, we've found the FireWire variety to be better suited to capturing video from a DV camcorder. USB drives require processing power from the computer, whereas Firewire drives are less processor-dependent.

One particular device we recommend is the ADS Pyro 1394/USB2.0 Drive Kit (www.adstech.com). You put the hard drives of your choice into these data tanks. Any hard drive can be dropped into the ADS drive kit, and it's plug-and-play. This is a great way to take your project from home and work on it at the office or while traveling with a laptop.

There are other hardware devices that can make your editing more pleasant and efficient. World Tech and Bella Keyboards both make keyboards made for video editing. Neither of these keyboards have any special function that will enable you to access "hidden" features in Vegas Movie Studio, but they have many keyboard shortcuts printed on the keys, and they are color coded. These keyboard shortcut codes apply to both Vegas Movie Studio and Vegas+DVD Architect, Sony's professional editing application.

Although not critical, the soundcard is an important part of any production system, whether it's a high-end system or a home-video editing system. Low-quality soundcards make it difficult to listen (monitor) audio with accuracy. This is fairly important if audio is a big part of your production. Therefore, a better-than-average soundcard is often a good add-on to any computer system. Low-cost soundcards can induce noise into the audio, and while the noise will not be heard in the finished product if the digital chain is maintained, it makes it difficult to accurately hear what is actual audio and what is being inserted as noise or changed quality by the soundcard.

Echo and M-Audio both make very affordable soundcards for use with typical home-editing systems. The Echo Mia and the M-Audio Sonica are both great alternatives to any built-in soundcard.

Good audio speakers are helpful as well. Although fine for playing games and listening to downloaded music, these sorts of speakers are not optimal for authoring video projects. Raw audio from a camcorder is uncompressed, which is very different from audio coming from a CD or downloaded music. In order to hear exactly what's coming from the camcorder, better speakers that aren't made of plastic are a good thing to look into. These Studiophile M-Audio LX4 2.1 Surround Sound Expandable Reference Monitors are very affordable and sound great. Add the LX4 5.1 Expander at any time to complete your full 5.1 surround sound system.

Setting your monitor properly is a good practice in order to enjoy great video with Vegas Movie Studio. The higher the resolution of your monitor, the more optimal your editing experience and preview of video will be. It's recommended that your monitor resolution never be less than 1024×768, while a higher setting of at least 1280×800 is highly suggested. To check your monitor resolution, right-click on your desktop and choose "Properties" and choose the "Settings" tab. This will allow you to reset your display properties if they are lower than the recommended settings.

There are other tweaks and improvements you can make to your computer that cost nothing and that will improve your performance significantly when editing video. One of the things that will improve the performance is to be sure your hard drive controllers are in what's called DMA or Direct Memory Access mode. To access this in Windows XP, go to Control Panel>System>Device Manager. Here you will find the IDE/ATAPI Controllers. If you double-click this controller, you'll see your Primary and Secondary drives. Double-click the drive and you'll see the Properties of that drive. Click on the Advanced tab in this dialog, and you'll have access to the drive transfer mode. In the drop-down menu, choose "DMA If Available" mode rather than PIO mode. This will allow faster access to memory. Have no fear; this cannot harm your system in any way.

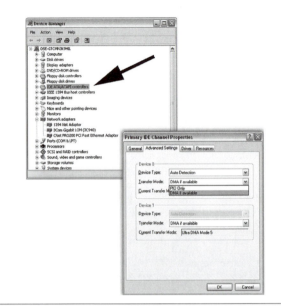

Repeat this process for your secondary drive.

Additional practices to keep in mind when editing video on a desktop or laptop computer are to:

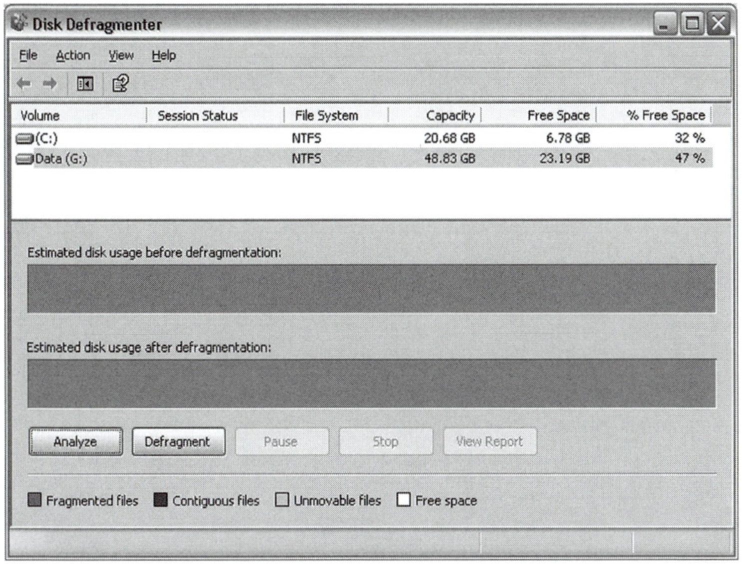

Disk Defragmenter

Volume	Session Status	File System	Capacity	Free Space	% Free Space
(C:)		NTFS	20.68 GB	6.78 GB	32 %
Data (G:)		NTFS	48.83 GB	23.19 GB	47 %

Estimated disk usage before defragmentation:

Estimated disk usage after defragmentation:

[Analyze] [Defragment] [Pause] [Stop] [View Report]

■ Fragmented files ■ Contiguous files □ Unmovable files □ Free space

Disable anti-virus and anti-spyware while editing video. (Consider creating a profile for video editing that has these applications disabled)

Keep background applications from running while editing video. If you are editing video, it's not a good practice to be checking email, listening to a CD, or other memory-stealing practices. Turn off all active applications in your system tray. If you do not know how to do this, there are Start Up memory information pages all across the Internet; check them out.

Defrag your hard drives often, particularly before starting any new video project. To defragment hard drives, go to "My Computer" and right-click the hard drive. You'll see a dialog that offers "Properties" as one of the choices. Select this option, and the window seen to the left will appear. Choose the Tools tab and defragment from that point. This will take a while for your computer to accomplish, so it's a good idea to do your defragmentation process during a time you don't expect to need the computer.

You can also find a useful function in

your drive properties that will clean up your hard drive. It will get rid of Internet files (if you use Internet Explorer), temporary files, and files in the recycle bin. If you use another browser, like Netscape or Firefox, you will need to find the cache or temporary files folder within Windows Explorer to delete the unnecessary files. Delete cookies in your Internet folder. You don't need them, and after a while you may have a lot of cookies just hanging out on your drive. Uninstall programs you don't use anymore. You're just wasting drive space when you could be using it for something else. Do this after you delete lots of files, use the Internet for a long time, or at least once a week.

Find and Clean Junk and Obsolete Files						

Check the boxes of the drive(s) you wish to scan.

☑ Local Disk (C:)
☐ MemoryStick (D:)
☐ Data (G:)

Actions
Stop
Exit

Name	Size	Type	Last Modified
C:\Documents and Settings\Spot\Application Data\Sony\... File meets search filter file-type criteria. (Temporary Files)	1 KB	TMP File	2/9/2005 9:03:14 PM
C:\Documents and Settings\Spot\Application Data\Sony\... File meets search filter file-type criteria. (Temporary Files)	1 KB	TMP File	2/9/2005 9:03:14 PM
C:\Documents and Settings\Spot\Desktop\Jody.veg.bak File meets search filter file-type criteria. (Temporary backup files)	58 KB	BAK File	2/3/2005 12:32:44 PM
C:\Documents and Settings\Spot\Desktop\MovieStudioFil... File meets search filter file-type criteria. (Temporary backup files)	12 KB	BAK File	2/24/2005 2:29:42 PM

Scanning: C:\Program Files\Common Files\CineForm\...

Finally, there is a product available called Enditall that you can find on the web. This application will help with video editing on home computers that have several processes in the background. Written by Niel Rubenking and found on the PCMag.com site, this free application will automatically close all processes not required by Windows to operate, freeing up valuable resources for your video editing system. As with installation of any application, be sure that you set a restore point on your computer prior to installing. This will allow you to roll back the computer system in the event that the application doesn't function the way you'd like it to.

Taking these small steps will help you enjoy the editing experience that much more and will go a long way towards ensuring a stable editing experience on the typical home computer.

Chapter 3

Getting the Good Stuff In

Now it's time to discuss the NLE workflow and how to import the media you need for your project, organize it, and prepare to start editing.

Workflow Can Be Fun!

Before you can begin using this powerful software NLE, it's helpful to understand the process, or workflow of building a video or audio project. There are three main steps: locate and manage all the parts and components of the project, bring them together into a coherent and appealing aural and visual experience, and output the finished project.

Locating resources:

- Gather the material you need (video, stills, graphics, etc.)

- "Log" or preview your video footage by watching the video and making notes

- Import or capture the video clips into the computer

- Import other media to the computer such as music from a CD or other resource

- Create or find other necessary material

Organize resources into a complete video:

- Arrange audio and video elements on the software Timeline

- Transition between these elements

- Add titles

- Edit the audio

- Add music, sound effects, and mix the audio

- Record, edit, and produce the audio in Sound Forge Audio Studio and ACID Music Studio

Render the final video or finish the audio project:

- Print to tape, burn a CD, burn a DVD, etc.

Project File Notes

Vegas Movie Studio uses project files. The application does not store media with its associated file but rather stores the "address" of any media found in the project. This means the media stays in place on your hard drives. The software only points to the media.

ACID Music Studio works the same way. Loops are never replicated or stored with the project; they are merely addressed. Sound Forge works on the exact file that is open in it but does not allow for saving of media as a project file, since there is no layering or multi-track capability in the application.

Understanding how both audio and video flow through a project may be helpful. Click Help>Show Me How. Vegas Movie Studio

NLE editing is also nondestructive. This means that all the work in your project file does not affect the actual media. It remains untouched in its original condition. Vegas Movie Studio works with the media, applying effects in real time but doesn't alter the media permanently.

If you use multiple external drives such as a FireWire drive, you may get these messages frequently depending on how drive letters get assigned. All your media may be on a D drive, but the next time you fire up the drive, it may be assigned drive letter G. Vegas Movie Studio will be looking on D for your media. Quickly point to the media now on G and continue working.

As a consequence, the project file must be rendered to apply all the project attributes—your hard work—to a finished file. This file is also separate from the original media.

If you delete or move the media, the program informs you what's missing when you reopen a project file. You have options for locating the media and updating the project.

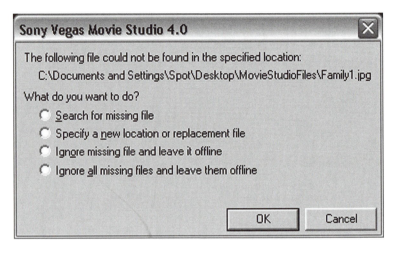

Starting a New Project in Vegas Movie Studio

Launch Vegas Movie Studio. There may be an icon on your desktop or simply point to the Windows Start menu>All Programs>Sony and continue to navigate to the program. You may also drag an icon to your Toolbar if you wish to have a QuickLaunch.

To start a new project, click File>New, click the New button on the Toolbar, or use the keyboard shortcut Ctrl+N.

The Project Properties dialog box displays. There are three tabs from which to choose: General, Folders, or Summary. Most of your work will be in the General tab.

The General tab displays the various video options. We suggest you choose a template from the drop-down box by clicking the arrow. The default, NTSC DV (720×480), 29.97fps, matches the video properties of miniDV camcorders; it's the best choice in this case. The PAL equivalent is the PAL DV (720×576), 25fps template. You can also modify these templates by checking the "Modify Template" checkbox, or you can auto-instruct Vegas Movie Studio to conform to the properties of the media that you'll import.

The Folders tab shows options for where you'll want temporary files to render to and for where your default media folders are to be located. Again, sticking with the defaults is fine for most instances. If you have a second drive for video use, point both of these to the temp video drive.

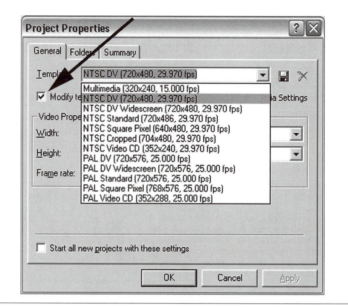

The Summary tab allows you to input information about the author, copyright, date of project, etc. This information will be auto-embedded in any stream you create and will show up in most media players if streaming media is authored.

Make sure you click OK to make any changes you made to the project properties apply. If you need to access the project properties again, click File> Properties or use the keyboard shortcut Alt+Enter.

After creating a new file, it's a really good idea to name it by saving it. See below.

Open, Close, Save, Save As

To open an existing project, click File>Open, click the Open button on the Toolbar, or use the keyboard shortcut Ctrl+O. Navigate to the file using the dialog box that displays and then click Open. It's a good idea to store your project files in one place or at least one folder per project.

If you customize any settings that you'd like to open all future projects with, check the "Start All New Projects With These Settings" box. Vegas Movie Studio will remember these settings and open all future projects with it.

If you have a second hard drive, point options in the Folders tab to the second hard drive. You'll have better overall performance.

Alternately, use the Explorer to locate the project file and click, drag, and drop it on the Timeline to open the existing project.

To save a project, click File>Save, click the Save button on the Toolbar, or use the keyboard shortcut Ctrl+S. Use the dialog box to name your project and also decide where it should reside on your computer.

Save As is useful for saving projects with new names. Click File>Save Project As to access the dialog. Since Vegas Movie Studio does not keep media with the project file, the file sizes are quite small. It can make real sense to save works in progress. This serves two purposes. One, you can experiment with different ideas and return to earlier versions. Two, you have a backup of your work should something happen to your original file. In other words, give files a name like "familyvideo_1.vf," "familyvideo_2.vf." This allows you to have various versions to go back to.

An asterisk (*) in the title bar (next to the file name) means there are unsaved changes in the current project. Make sure you save projects periodically. Get in the habit of using Ctrl+S to save the project.

We can't emphasize enough the importance of backups! Use the 2x2 rule: two copies in two different places (different hard drives, computers, CD, etc.).

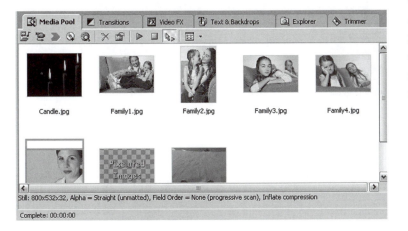

Another terrific feature of the Save Project As dialog is for packaging projects. When you've finished a project, click File>Save Project As. Give your project a final name and navigate to the folder to hold it. Put a check in the box "Copy and trim media with project" and click Save.

To Media Pool or Not to Media Pool

The choice of using the Media Pool or not to organize your projects is up to you. The Media Pool is like a "catch-all" where you can always find any piece of media you've used in the project. You can import all project media to the Media Pool in one shot, or you can import media to the Timeline from the Explorer, and Vegas Movie Studio will place a reference (not a copy) of the media on the Timeline in the Media Pool.

Click the Import Media button in the Media Pool to locate media you want to import to the project. You cannot import folders; you'll need to import the media files in groups or as individual files.

Organize media in folders before starting the project, putting all your video into one folder, photos in another, audio in another, stored in a master folder or directory.

You may find it more efficient to organize media in a project folder and then access the folder from the Explorer. This is how most video editors work in the professional world.

Import Media

To add media to the Media Pool, have it open and then click the Import Media button or choose File>Import media.

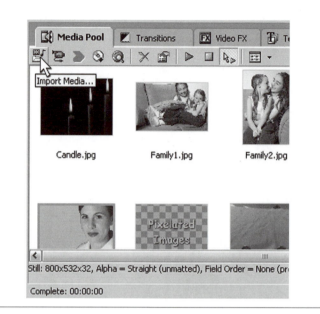

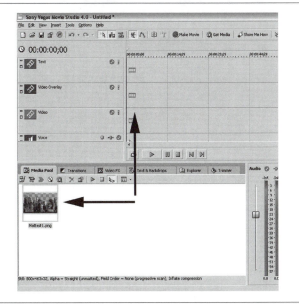

Use the dialog box to navigate to the media and click Open.

Notice the file is added to the media bin but not the project Timeline.

Change how files display in the Media Pool by clicking the Views button and making a selection. Choose from Lists, Details, or thumbnails. If you have a slower video card or older computer, use Lists or Details for best results.

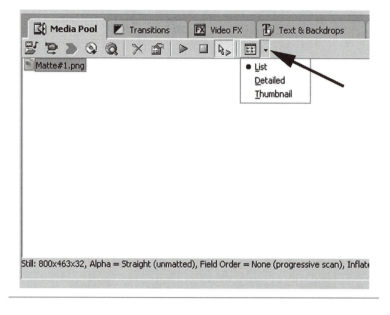

If the files you are importing are on removable media, such as stock video footage on a CD-ROM, consider moving the files to a folder on the hard drive before importing the clips into the Media Pool. Otherwise, if remove the CD, the files will be unavailable for your project.

Capturing Video Workflow

There are several workflow approaches when capturing video.

Capture everything—With this approach, you capture entire tapes (usually as one long file). Then, use the Trimmer Tool to slice and dice the video. Markers and regions will help you organize the clips in the Trimmer.

Automatic scene detection—This approach captures entire tapes with "Enable DV scene detection" turned on (it is by default). Instead of one long file, the software chops up the file based on scene changes (basically when the camcorder was stopped and started during shooting). Scene detection only works for DV devices and if you have a date and time set in your DV camera.

Advanced Capture—This technique means going through the tape manually and setting in-points and out-points for the clips you want to use. After logging these selections, Vegas automatically captures the clips.

Manual—With this method, watch the tape and capture clips manually as they play. This is what you'll need to do if you are working with a non-DV camera or video source.

Logging

You must watch your footage carefully to see what you really have. If you are editing video that somebody else shot, this step is critical. This is called logging and can be done before, during, or after capture. Logging is simply taking notes about what footage you have at a specific time on the tape and determining which shots you'd like to use.

- *Before* lets you focus on the video and not worry about technical issues. Hook up the camcorder to a TV, curl up on the couch, watch, and take notes.

- *During* means watching, evaluating, and capturing at the same time. Coupled to advanced capture, this approach can make for efficient capture sessions.

- *After* means getting the clips into the computer first and then logging the material. This is a fine approach for shorter projects. For longer projects where you'll be using much of what you shot, such as a training video, this can work, too. However, for a long documentary, where you shot 50 hours of tape, you may want to consider a hybrid of the before/during method, only capturing the footage you feel you'll use.

Take some notes while you watch, describing the footage, its quality, and even possible ideas as to how it will all cut together. At first, do this with paper, but as you rack up more editing time, you'll be surprised how easy this is to do in your head. Working from a written script outline always helps.

Hooking Up the Gear

Capturing from a DV camcorder requires an OHCI-compliant 1394 port on your computer. Called i.LINK® by Sony or as it's more popularly known, FireWire. With the camcorder turned off, connect its FireWire output to the computer input. This usually requires a four-pin to six-pin cable for desktops and four-pin to four-pin for connecting to a laptop. If you use a DV deck instead of a camcorder, use its FireWire output.

Turn on the camcorder or deck, and Windows should recognize the device. Close this Windows dialog box at this point. Typically the camcorder should be in VCR mode, not camera (check your camcorder's documentation for details).

Vegas Movie Studio supports capturing "live" from a DV source. Switch to camera mode and the current picture displays ready for capture. Be aware that the audio picked up by the camera mic may feed back through your computer speakers, so turn them down first. Obviously, you must capture manually (video or stills) with this technique. This is a great method of capturing a church service or school event where time is sensitive and you need to accomplish an SDE (same-day edit).

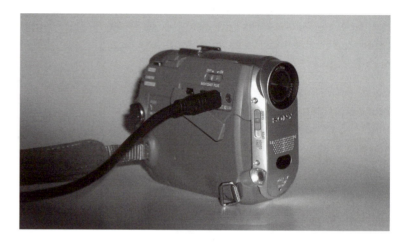

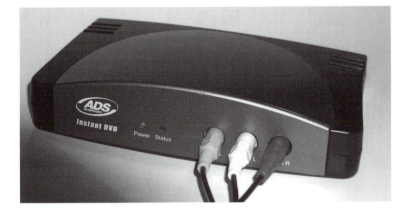

To capture analog video either connect the analog source, such a VHS to a camcorder or to an external capture device, such as the ADS Pyro A/V Link. Connect the camcorder or ADS to the computer via its FireWire connection, turn it on, and proceed.

Basic Capture

With the Media Pool open, click the Capture video button or use File> Capture Video to launch the Video Capture utility. The Verify Tape Name dialog displays. Enter a name for the tape.

To help prevent dropping frames during capture, reduce the size of the capture window to a very small size. Also, turn off or temporarily disable background applications, such as an Internet connection and anti-virus utilities. Capture moves a lot of data between the camcorder and the computer. It's best not to let anything interfere with that formidable task. Defragmenting the capture hard drive before the session will often improve capture performance.

Verify Tape Name ? X

Please verify that the tape name displayed below is correct for the current tape. Otherwise, choose the correct tape name from the drop-down list or type a new name in the box.

Tape name: | Tape 1 | ▾

◉ Don't capture any clips right now

○ Start capturing all clips from the current tape position

○ Start capturing all clips from the beginning of the tape

[OK] [Cancel]

The capture utility has three main tabs: Capture, Advanced Capture, and Print to Tape. There is also a Preview window with transports controls. Along the bottom, the Clip Explorer functions like the Media Pool.

Note: Print to Tape is explained later in this book.

Before capturing clips, click Options> Preferences>Disk Management.

If the screen says "Please connect a device" double-check the connections. If that seems fine, try cycling the camcorder off and then back on again. If all is well, the screen should read "Device connected."

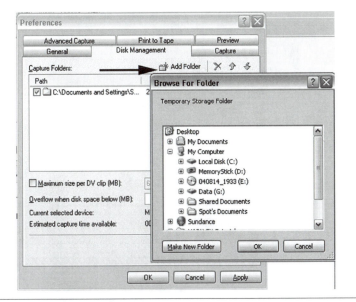

Determine where to store the captured files. It's recommended that you have a dedicated media hard drive separate from the C drive. Click the "Add Folder" button and use the dialog box to indicate this capture location. Create a new folder, if needed, by clicking the "Make New Folder" button. Click OK to close the dialog box.

You can create many capture folders and activate them by placing a check mark adjacent to the path. To deactivate a folder, remove the check mark. To delete a folder, click the "Remove Selected Folder" button or just press Delete on the keyboard. Whenever possible, capture to a separate hard drive.

Notice the available free space indicator and the Estimated capture time available. Use this information to plan your capture locations. The format is hours:minutes:seconds;frames.

Since the Sony Video Capture is a separate program, save your sessions using File>Save.

With the Preferences dialog box still open, switch to the Capture tab (Options>Preferences>Capture). Clear the checkbox "Enable DV scene detection" if you wish to turn this feature off (it is on by default). DV scene detection will attempt to capture scene changes to individual files. This is handy when working with long files but not usable when using advanced capture.

With a DV device connected, notice that there is remote control over its transport functions: Play, Pause, Stop, Step backward left, Step forward right, Rewind, Fast-forward. There is also a scrubber control.

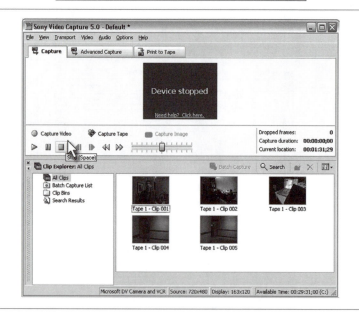

Above the transport controls are three choices: Capture Video, Capture Tape, and Capture Image.

Capture Video—This is the equivalent of a Record button. Simply play the tape and click this button to record what you see on screen. Click Stop to quit capturing.

The Capture Complete dialog box displays important information about the capture session, including whether you dropped, or lost, any frames.

- Show Clips—displays thumbnails of what you captured

- Rename All—changes the base name of the clips

- Delete All—removes the clips captured

- Done—accepts the clips and adds them to the Clip Bin. Check the box to add the captured clips to the Media Pool, too.

Capture Tape—Click this to capture the entire tape in one session. The software rewinds the tape, if necessary, and records everything on the tape. Consider enabling DV scene detection in Preferences (as explained above) to automatically chop the tape into shorter chunks. The Capture Complete dialog displays at the end of this session, too.

If you get dropped frames, you may need to recapture. Unfortunately, the software doesn't tell you where those lost frames are. You'll have to manually hunt them down. My method of working is to simply redo the capture if dropped frames are indicated, but you'll want to find out the cause of the dropped frames first.

Be aware that blank spaces on the tape can confuse the Capture Tape setting into thinking the tape is over. If you have these gaps caused by not stopping and restarting the tape in the same place, you may need to capture manually.

Capture Image—Navigate to the still you want to capture on the tape and click Capture Image. Vegas and Screenblast capture a still to the JPEG file format.

If you prefer to save stills as bitmaps (BMP), use Options>Preferences>Capture and clear the "Save captured stills as JPEG" checkbox.

To automatically deinterlace captured stills, check the "Deinterlace image when capturing stills" checkbox in Options>Preferences>Capture.

Use Capture Still for stop-motion animation and time-lapse sequences. Vegas Movie Studio captures and sequentially numbers individual frames. Later you can import this image sequence as one event on the Timeline. This feature is great for creating clay-mation type animations.

Advanced Capture

There are many benefits to using the Advanced Capture features. One, you can log tapes and capture only those shots you deem worthy. Two, you can batch capture after creating the capture list. Three, you can easily recapture media in the future provided that you save the Video Capture file.

Click the Advanced Capture tab to access the controls. If the Verify Tape Name dialog displays, enter a name for the tape.

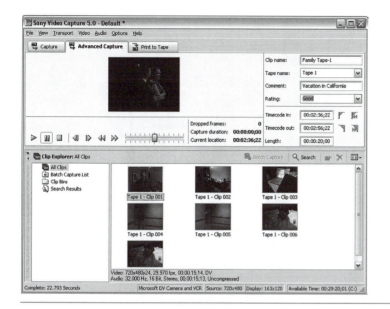

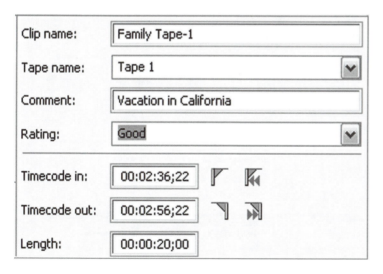

The screen looks essentially the same except for the new section to the right. With Advance Capture, you manually scrub the tape, locate the clips you want, name them, enter the clip's start (in) and finish (out) point, and then log these data. This builds the Batch Capture list for automatic, unattended capture. Alternatively, you can immediately capture the clip manually.

Avoid capturing clips exactly where you plan to edit them. Instead leave some handles, or extra time, at the beginning and ending of each clip. In short, your clip in-points and out-points should be rather loose.

Use the transport controls to locate the start of the clip you wish to capture.

- Clip name: Enter a name for the clip. The software suggests a name based on the tape name and the clip number (which sequentially number automatically). Accept these defaults or enter a more meaningful name.

- Tape name: Choose the tape currently in the camcorder.

- Comment: Enter an optional note about the clip.

- Rating: Choose a rating from the drop-down list.

Click the Mark In button or use the I keyboard shortcut.

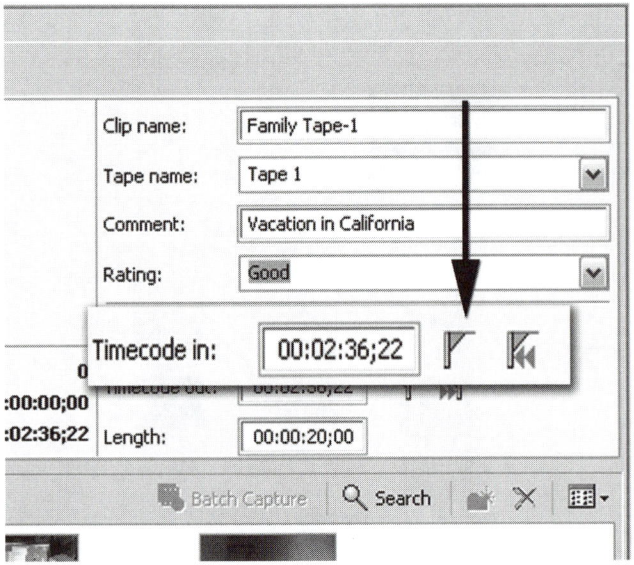

Navigate to the end of the clip and click the Mark Out button or use the O keyboard shortcut. Notice that the length of the clip displays.

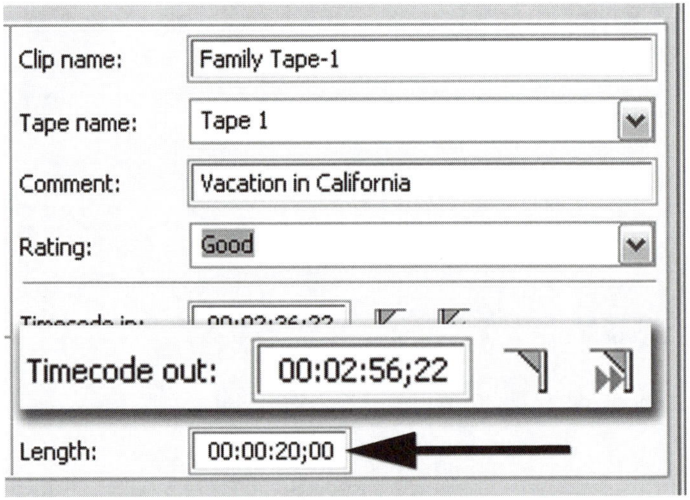

It's acceptable to enter a clip's out-point before its in-point.

Clip name:	Family Tape-1
Tape name:	Tape 1
Comment:	Vacation in California
Rating:	Good

Timecode in: 00:02:36;22

:00:00;00
:02:36;22   Length: 00:00:20;00

Batch Capture   Search

Clip name:	Family Tape-1
Tape name:	Tape 1
Comment:	Vacation in California
Rating:	Good

Timecode out: 00:02:56;22

Length: 00:00:20;00

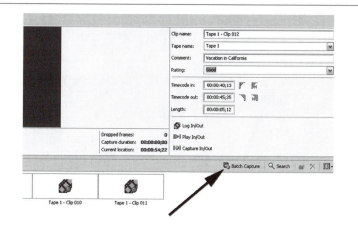

After setting the in-point and out-point, there are three choices:

- Log In/Out—Adds the clip to the Batch Capture List

- Play In/Out—Plays the clip

- Capture In/Out—Captures the clip immediately

Continue to log your tape or tapes, repeating the above workflow until finished.

If you choose to batch capture your tape, click the Batch Capture button in the Clip Explorer right pane to initiate the capture process after you've created the list.

Vegas will start the capture process. This works automatically and doesn't require your attention. The Capture Complete dialog box displays when the batch process finishes so you can check for any errors.

When using Advanced Capture, save and name the session. Should you need to recapture clips, simply recall the file, put in the appropriate tape, and start the batch capture again.

Scanning Photographs and Other Graphics

Many videos use still images and graphics to tell their story. To get this pre-existing media into your computer, you'll need a flatbed scanner and its associated software installed.

With the Media Pool open, and a bin created and selected, click the Get photo button or File>Get photo to launch your scanning software.

Refer to your scanner's instructions for specific details.

Example Olympus Twain Scanner software

Though you can use any supported file format, we suggest saving files using the PNG format for best results.

Computers use square pixels, while DV uses rectangles (.909 of square). If you prepare media in a photo editing or other graphics program, resize them to 720×576 (PAL: 704×576) to compensate for the NLE's square-to-rectangle conversion. Double that size if you plan to zoom in on the graphic. Vegas Movie Studio is capable of correcting for aspect-ratio issues if you wish to do it in the application.

Saving to PNG is again the best choice as the format supports alpha channel information which Vegas Movie Studio can recognize. Alpha channels are clear or transparent backgrounds which make compositing them over video a snap. PNG files are an ideal format for logos, lower thirds, and other effects. If you know a file has a transparent channel and it's not seen on the Timeline, right-click the media and choose Media Properties. In this dialog you'll be able to instruct Vegas Movie Studio to recognize the transparent channel.

Video's resolution is 72dpi, so it doesn't make sense to scan photographs or graphics at any resolution higher than 150dpi unless you are working with pictures smaller than 4 inches.

Media with an alpha channel has a gray checkerboard background in both the Media Pool and the Timeline.

Extract Audio from CD

Enable Auto-Preview in the Media Pool so that when you click a file, it automatically begins to play.

If you have purchased sound effects or production library music that comes on audio CDs, insert the disc, create or select a Media Pool bin, and click the Extract Audio from CD button or choose File>Extract Audio from CD.

Be sure to check out Acid Planet for other free media opportunities as well as for purchase.

From the dialog box, select choices from the Action drop-down list. Options include extracting individual tracks. Hold the Ctrl button to select multiple tracks.

The files will be automatically placed in the Media Pool.

Get Media from the Web

The last button in the Media Pool, Get Media from the Web, launches your web browser and takes you to a special section of the Sony web site. Here you can download free media along with links to media for sale.

Track	Type	Start	End	Length
01	Audio	00:02.00	04:17.57	04:15.57
02	Audio	04:17.57	08:48.07	04:30.25
03	Audio	08:48.07	12:49.10	04:01.03
04	Audio	12:49.10	16:47.43	03:58.33
05	Audio	16:47.43	21:09.10	04:21.42
06	Audio	21:09.10	24:43.55	03:34.45
07	Audio	24:43.55	29:13.34	04:29.54
08	Audio	29:13.34	33:56.35	04:43.01
09	Audio	33:56.35	37:31.04	03:34.44
10	Audio	37:31.04	43:25.60	05:54.56
11	Audio	43:25.60	47:57.53	04:31.68
12	Audio	47:57.53	52:31.00	04:33.22
13	Audio	52:31.00	57:24.41	04:53.41

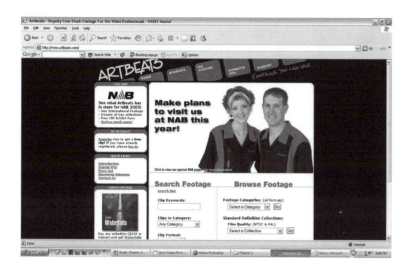

Adding Third-Party Material

Stock footage, such as the Artbeats collections used in this book, along with animations and other video eye candy work well in Vegas Movie Studio. Typically, this material arrives on CD-ROMs or DVD-ROMs ready to use. We suggest copying the files to the hard drive before adding them to your projects for best playback performance.

Artbeats Stock Footage Collection

Chapter 4

Cutting Up!

It's time to start building your project by adding media to the Timeline, creating audio and video tracks, and learning some basic editing techniques.

Though video and audio reside on separate tracks, the software treats them equally as events. Vegas Movie Studio calls anything on the Timeline an "event." The principles discussed in this chapter apply whether it is a video or audio event. Where they differ, it will be so noted.

Adding Tracks and Media to the Timeline

Vegas Movie Studio offers three video tracks and three audio channels (tracks). The track on top always takes priority over the lower tracks. Even though these tracks are labeled as Text, Overlay, or Video, they may be used for any kind of video or graphic media.

Add media to the Timeline using either the Media Pool, Explorer, or Trimmer. The Media Pool and Explorer work similarly. Left-click to select the file, hold down the mouse button, drag the file to the applicable track on the Timeline, and release the mouse button. Also, use Shift+Click and/or Ctrl+Click to select and add multiple media files.

Double-clicking a file in Explorer or Media Pool using the left mouse button will also add it to the selected track at the current cursor position.

Put photos on the Overlay track if you find yourself running out of track layer options.

When you add multiple files to the Timeline all at once, they will be placed in alphanumeric order. However, note that the actual file you drag will be placed first.

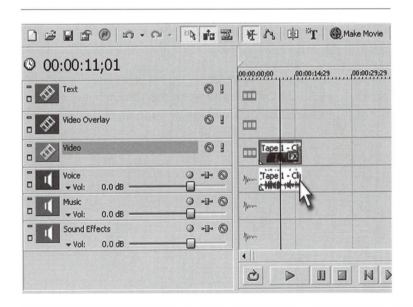

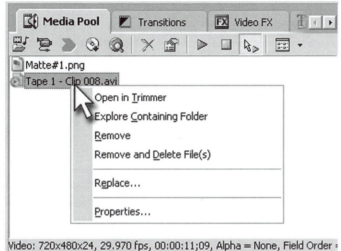

If a video file has audio associated with it, the audio will be added to its corresponding audio track automatically.

To move a file to the Trimmer, right-click the media file in Explorer and choose either "Open in Trimmer" (or "Add to Media Pool"). Again, it's usually best to build your project folders prior to starting the project, so you shouldn't need to add files to the media pool.

Right-click a file in the Media Pool and choose "Open in Trimmer" and the file will open in the Trimmer. If you've inserted regions or markers in the Trimmer in a previous editing session, the Trimmer will display the regions or markers.

Vegas Movie Studio editors use the Trimmer for two main reasons:

- To fine-tune, or trim, the edges of a media event.

- To add multiple shorter sections from a longer event to the project, for example, splitting the best parts from a single long interview into a more specific segment.

Use the Trimmer to cut out or locate scenes from a long file captured from a VHS or other non-digital source.

You do *not* have to use the Trimmer. Vegas Movie Studio allows trimming and splitting events on the Timeline. See below.

Before adding a file to the Timeline using the Trimmer, make a time selection. There are two methods.

Play the clip and press I for the in-point or start point and then press O for the out-point or stop point. Notice the bar along the top of the Trimmer window. Double-click this time selection to select it. Blue lines appear at the ends.

The other method is to position the cursor above the Trimmer ruler and click and drag a time selection.

Once you've made a time selection, click the media inside the selection and drag it to the Timeline. Alternately, click the Add Media from Cursor button or use the A keyboard shortcut. This puts the media time selection on the selected track at the cursor position going forward.

Use the "R" key to create regions in the Trimmer. The Trimmer will remember your regions when you reopen the same file in the Trimmer.

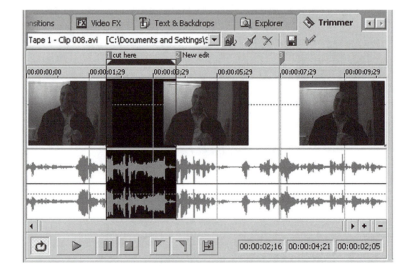

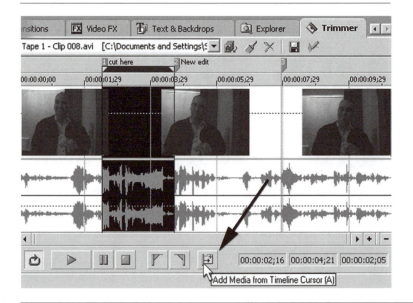

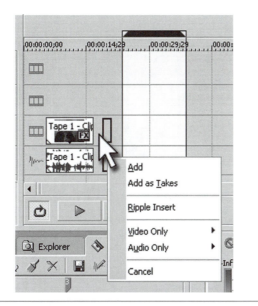

Right-Click Add Media Options

There is additional power when dragging files from Explorer, Media Pool, or Trimmer using a right mouse button click-and-drag. Select a media file using either Explorer, Media Pool, or Trimmer. Press and hold the right mouse button and drag to the Timeline. A dialog box pops up.

The results of these options vary depending on whether you add a single file or multiple files.

Right-click add single media file options:

- Add—places the event along the Timeline forward.

- Add as Takes—places the event along the Timeline forward (see below)

- Ripple Insert—Slides media forward in time to make room for the new file

- Video Only—performs one of the above operations for only the video portion of a file

- Audio Only—performs one of the above operations for only the audio portion of a file

- Cancel

Here's yet another method. Right-click media in the Vegas Trimmer and select from the options:

Select a track and then make a time selection on the Timeline. Switch to the Trimmer and click the Add Media from Cursor button to fill the Timeline time selection with the media from the Trimmer. This is called "fit-to-fill" editing and is usually found only on more-expensive NLE applications.

- Select Video and Audio

- Select Video Only (Tab)

- Select Audio Only (Shift+Tab)

Then, use the Add Media from Cursor or Add Media up to Cursor button.

Moving Events

Move an event on the Timeline by selecting it and dragging it into position.

<u>C</u>opy	Ctrl+C
● Select V<u>i</u>deo and Audio	
Select Vi<u>d</u>eo Only	Tab
Select <u>A</u>udio Only	Shift+Tab
Video Height <u>L</u>arger	Ctrl+Shift+Up
● Video and Audio E<u>q</u>ual Height	
Audio Height Lar<u>g</u>er	Ctrl+Shift+Down
<u>M</u>arker	M
<u>R</u>egion	R
Sa<u>v</u>e Markers/Regions	S
A<u>u</u>to-Save Trimmer Markers/Regions	Shift+S
Sy<u>n</u>c Track View Selection Time from Cursor	T
Syn<u>c</u> Track View Selection Time up to Cursor	Shift+T
<u>Z</u>oom Selection	Ctrl+Up
Add Media <u>f</u>rom Cursor	A
Add Media u<u>p</u> to Cursor	Shift+A

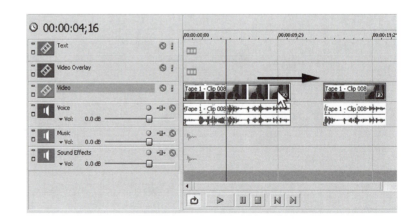

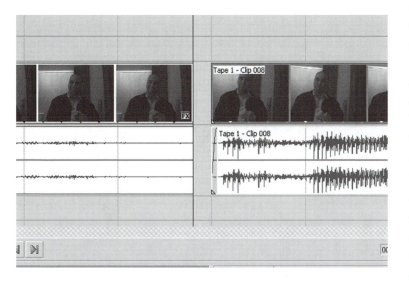

Butt one event right next to another for a straight or butt cut. Use care to not leave tiny gaps between events. Zoom in closer to be sure your edits are accurate. Use the up and down arrow keys to zoom in and out on the Timeline or use your mouse wheel. In this image, you can see a one-frame gap. This will blink as a black frame, so it's not a good thing.

You can cut, copy, and paste Timeline events, too.

To avoid this issue, enable snapping by either clicking the Toolbar icon or using Options>Enable Snapping (F8). Make sure Snap to Frames, Snap to Grid, and Snap to Markers are enabled, too.

Timeline Trimming and Splitting

To change the start and end points of a piece of media, select the event on the Timeline by clicking it. The upper and lower edges of the media will fill with a green color.

Position the cursor at either edge. Notice how the cursor changes. Click and drag in to shorten events; click and drag out to lengthen events.

Vegas shows the edge frame in the Preview window as you trim the event.

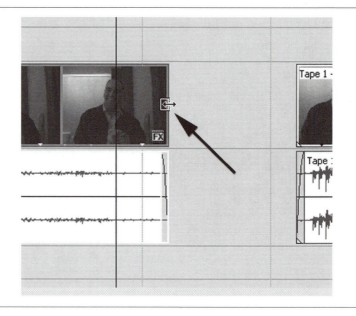

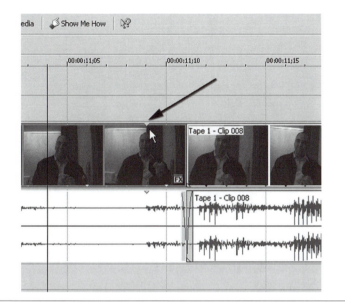

If you drag an event past its end, the event starts over or loops. The tiny divot at the top of the event indicates the loop point.

Right-click the video file and choose Switches>Loop. Now when you drag an event past its end point, the last frame holds for as long as you extend the event. Note that the loop divot still appears.

We prefer to leave looping enabled. To override this global setting, right-click the event and choose Properties. In the dialog box, uncheck the loop checkbox and click OK. This event will no longer loop (and instead hold its last frame when extended). This is one method of creating a freeze-frame in Vegas Movie Studio.

To break a larger event into two pieces, position the cursor where you want to split the event. Click Edit>Split or use the handy keyboard shortcut S.

Need to duplicate *and* move an event? Select it and hold down the Ctrl key while you drag the copied event to a new position. The original remains in place.

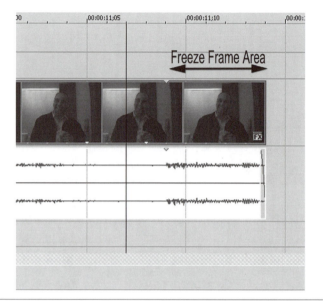

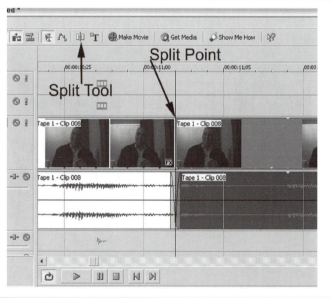

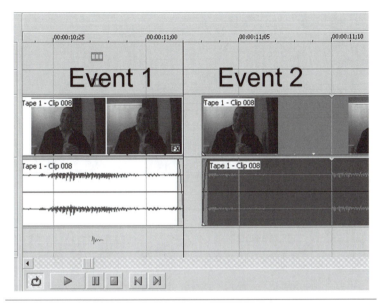

There are now two separate events.

Split events into as many pieces as needed. These separate events can be moved, copied, deleted and more—just as any other event.

Remember that NLE editing is non-destructive. Trimming, splitting, and other effects do not affect the original files in any way. They remain intact on the computer.

Envelopes and Events

Each event has its own envelope that control several features. Video event envelopes include fade in, fade out, opacity, and velocity. Audio event envelopes include fade in, fade out, and event volume level.

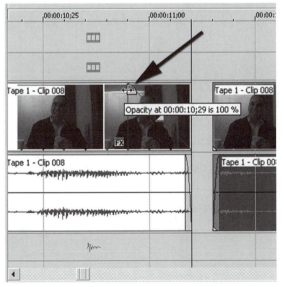

Video and Audio

Select an event on the Timeline. This can be a text, still, video, or audio event. Position the cursor near the top-left edge. Notice that the cursor changes to a pie shape with arrows.

Hold the mouse button and drag to the right. This adds a fade-in. Note the white line that shows the end of the fade-in and the quarter circle that indicates the slope of the fade.

Position the cursor near the top-right edge of the same event. Note the cursor change.

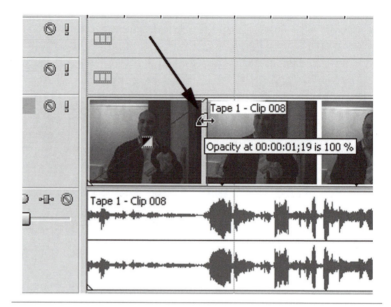

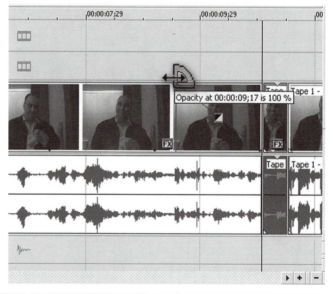

Hold the mouse button and drag to the left to add a fade-out.

Right-click either fade and choose Fade Type from the pop-up menu. Select from the choices to affect how the fade envelope progresses over time.

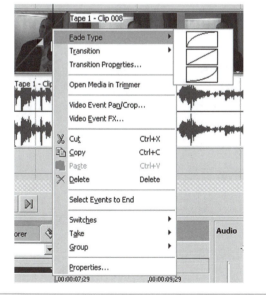

Next, position the cursor near the top of the video or audio event (away from the fades). The cursor changes to a pointing hand.

Click and drag down to change the opacity of the event. This allows a top event to superimpose over another event on a lower track; the lower track shows, too. This type of superimposition is known as compositing and is one of the techniques that allow you to be very creative and artistic. Notice the two images of the girls over the top of each other.

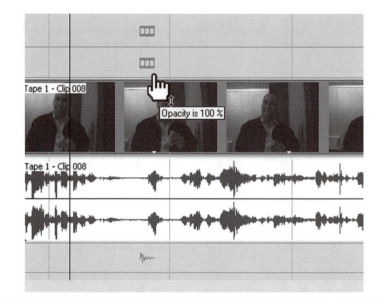

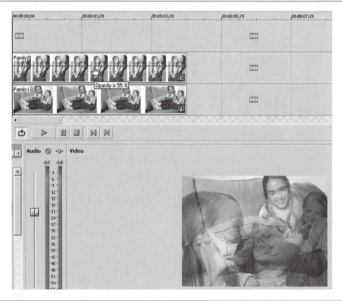

Transitions

Vegas Movie Studio will automatically crossfade any audio or video event dragged over the top of each other. These crossfades form a transition. Vegas Movie Studio offers a wide number of transitional tools.

Move one event so it overlaps another on the Timeline. Notice the X that appears, signifying a crossfade.

Play the Timeline to see how one event fades out while the other fades in. If this is an audio event, listen for the change.

The amount of event overlap determines the transition's time length.

Video events can have a variety of transitions applied to the crossfades. Click the Transitions tab in the Windows docking area at the bottom of the Vegas Movie Studio workspace. There are dozens of transitions from which to choose.

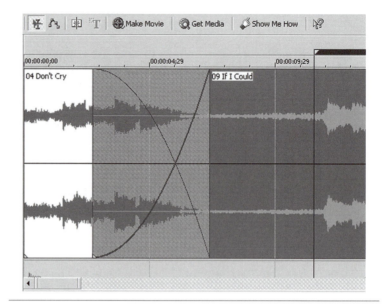

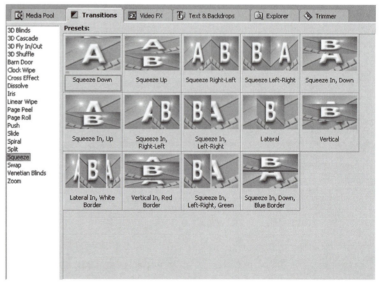

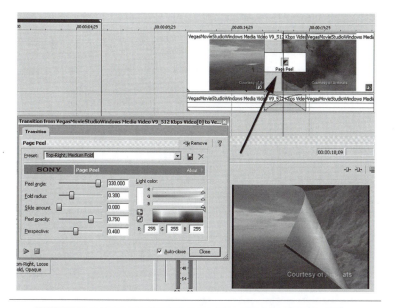

Click a transition, drag, and drop it on the crossfade created above.

The dialog box that displays provides control over the transition's properties. You can preview the transition by clicking the Play button in the lower-left corner of the dialog box. Make any necessary changes, then close the dialog box.

Create a looping region on the Timeline and let the video play back while you adjust the various properties of the transition dialog.

Click Play to preview the result.

Experiment by trying out other transitions to see how they look with your video.

Use Auto-Close to automatically close the dialog box when you click outside the dialog box, such as on the Timeline.

Transitions are *not* relegated for use only between events. You can add a fade-in or fade-out to a single event. Drag a transition and drop it on the fade to apply it to the single event.

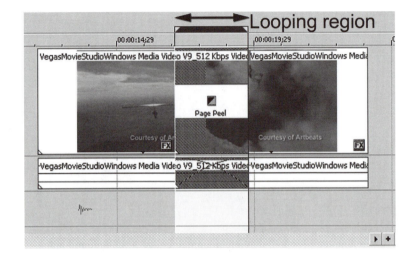

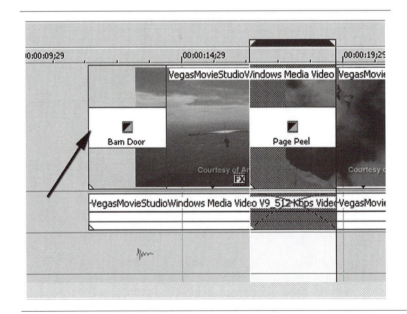

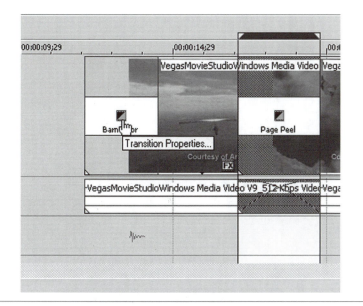

Click the icon in the middle of the transition, and the Transition dialog will reopen, allowing you to modify the parameters of the transition.

Right-click the Transition, choose Fade Type, and then select from the graphics which envelopes you want to use. Experiment to understand the differences. You might be surprised at what a difference various envelopes can make in the overall appearance of the crossfade.

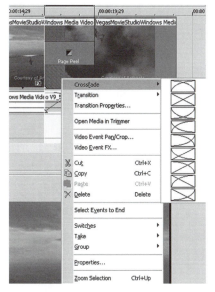

Slip Trim Events

Often there is a video clip event that is the right length on the Timeline, but you want to adjust where it starts and ends *within* the clip. Or you need to trim one edge, leaving the opposite edge anchored in place. This technique of determining the in-point and out-point is called slip trimming and is found in most professional video editing applications.

Select an event and hover the cursor over it. Don't hover over the cursor/playback indicator. Press and hold the Alt button. The mouse pointer changes to a box with two arrows in it. Left-click the mouse button and drag (while still pressing Alt).

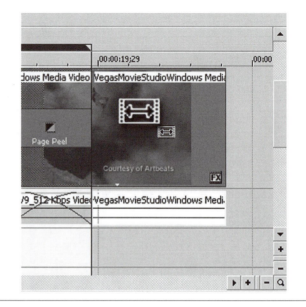

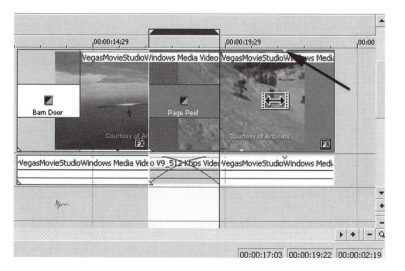

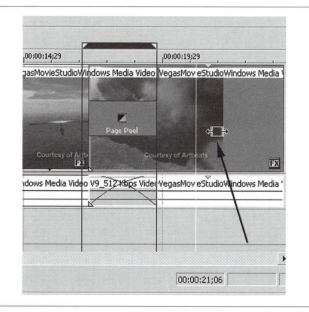

The video preview will display a small caret or divot in the top. This shows the event ending point. The event stays in place, but the video within changes. Be aware that if the divot appears in the middle of your Timeline, your video clip's beginning will show right after the ending point. The point displayed in the Preview window is the new in-point, and the divot will indicate the end of the event. Be sure to trim the event backwards to the divot point.

To slip trim one edge, click the event, press and hold Alt, and drag.

As you hold the Alt key and drag, one edge remains fixed, while the other slip trims.

To both move and slip trim an event, hold down Ctrl+Alt while dragging the event. This is difficult to do in Vegas Movie Studio, simply because you won't see the Preview window update as you slip trim.

Slip trims work best on clips that have already been edge trimmed. Slip trimming a whole event may introduce a loop point, indicated by the divot in the top of the video event.

Ripple Editing

Sometimes you need one edit to affect everything else after it. In other words, you want the edit to ripple down the Timeline. For example, you want to paste a new event between two existing ones with the whole project sliding down to make room. Ripple edit mode to the rescue. Ripple is a great feature, once you get used to the operation and function of the tool.

Turn on Auto Ripple by clicking the Toolbar icon or using the keyboard shortcut Ctrl+L.

Ripple edits work when using cut, copy, and paste on the Timeline. Ripple insert is also an option when you right-click add media file. The ripples affect only events on one selected track, though.

With an existing project displaying at least two events, delete one and watch the other events slide backward.

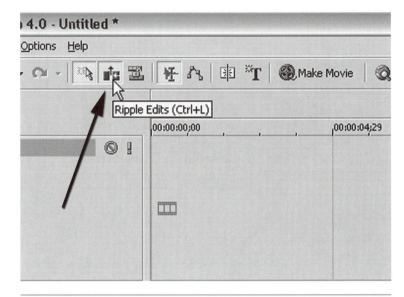

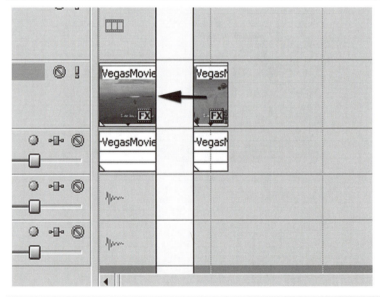

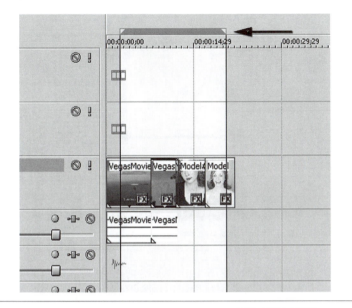

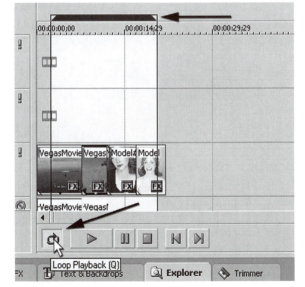

If you leave the Auto Ripple off, Vegas Movie Studio lets you perform a post edit ripple as well. This is great for rough-building a project by throwing media up on the Timeline and then rippling to delete holes left between the media.

Build the rough edits by placing media on the Timeline in the order you'd like them to appear. This is similar to storyboarding. Double-click the area between video events. With Ripple enabled, press Delete or Ctrl+X key. This will delete the hole between events and slide events backward in time to butt up against the previous event.

Time Selections

Click and drag above the ruler to make a time selection.

Click the Loop icon in the Transport section or use the Q shortcut to toggle looping on and off. Looping is a great feature, as it allows you to preview edits and filters as they take place.

The time selection changes colors to dark blue. Position the cursor inside the selection and click Play. The section will repeat endlessly until stopped.

Double-click an event to create a time selection exactly to size.

Double-click a transition to create a time selection the length of the transition. This is useful for checking the transition's duration ensuring uniformity for certain projects. It's also a great way to set up a loop to preview transitions while you audition them.

Vegas Movie Studio remembers the last five time selections. Use the Backspace key to cycle through them.

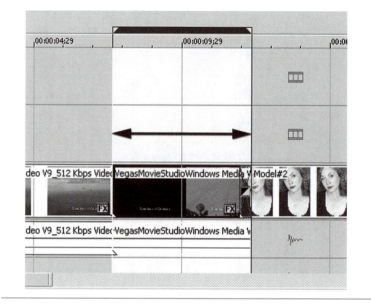

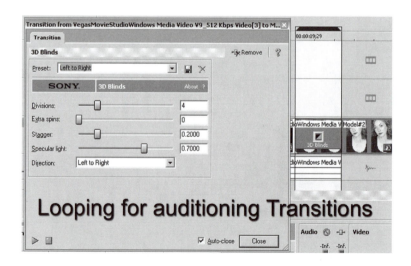

Looping for auditioning Transitions

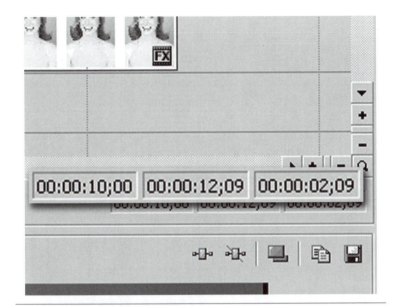

Below the Timeline, to the far right of the transport controls, are three boxes. The first indicates the start of the time selection; the second the end. The third shows the duration of the selection.

Double-click any of the boxes and type a value as needed.

If there is no time selection, the first box indicates the cursor position. Double-click and type a value to quickly move the cursor. Ctrl+G quickly highlights the box for data entry, too.

Markers and Regions

Time selections are temporary and ever-evolving. Use markers and regions as more permanent indicators. Markers and regions are the NLE equivalent of sticky notes. They appear just above the time selection area at the top of the Timeline.

Make a time selection and click Insert> Region or press R. Type a name for the region and press Enter.

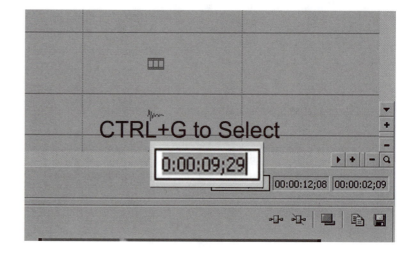

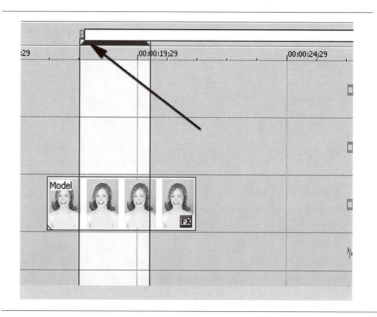

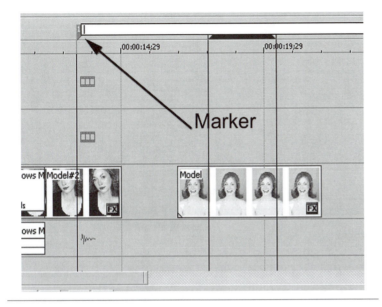

Marker

To mark a single point in time, position the cursor and press M to insert a marker. Give it a name and press Enter.

To move a marker, or either edge of a region, click and drag it to the new position.

Right-click a marker or region for additional options.

Markers can be inserted while a project plays in real time, too.

Jump right to one of the first 10 markers and regions by using the corresponding 1-0 keys on the keyboard (not the keypad).

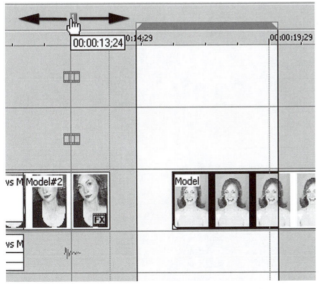

If you are capturing analog media using an i.Link converter device, it's a good technique to open the full length file in the Trimmer, create regions in the Trimmer, and save those regions out to be added to the Timeline later.

Organize your Timeline with regions too, using regions or markers as "sticky notes" to yourself, reminding yourself of text, images, or anything else that needs to be inserted.

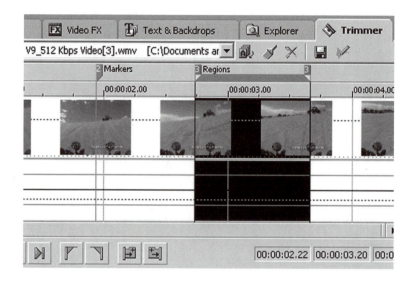

Chapter 5

Advanced Editing Techniques

In the last chapter, we looked at some basic editing techniques. There are a large number of creative tools available in Vegas Movie Studio, and they are there to let the artist in you shine. These include effects, compositing, picture-in-picture looks, movement on stills, and more.

Video FX

Video FX fall into two categories: utility and creative. Generally, utility effects fix something wrong with your video or audio. Creative effects typically take your project to a new level. However, some effects can be used both ways. Sometimes effects are referred to as "filters." There is no right or wrong word for describing these.

Video Effects

You can place Video FX on individual video events or the entire project. To place an effect, select it from the Video FX window found under the Video FX tab, click and drag, and drop it on the video event you'd like to affect. You can also drag the Video FX to the Preview window; this will apply FX to all video in the project, including titles, stills, and video.

The Video FX dialog displays, allowing you to tweak parameters of the specific effect you've chosen.

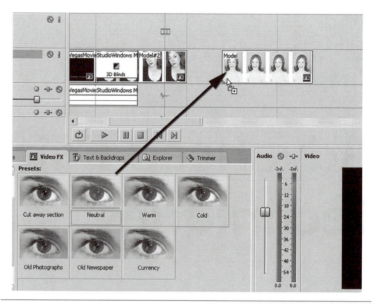

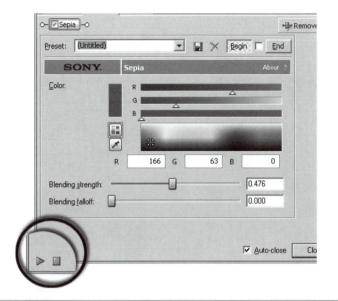

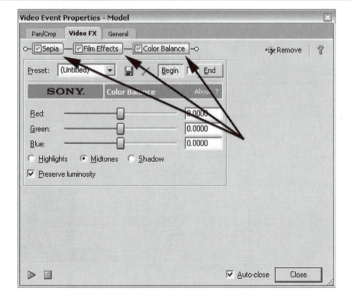

Adjust the parameters to suit your preference by moving the sliders until the video image looks as you'd like it to. You might need to move the dialog box to a new location on the computer monitor so you can see your changes taking place in the Preview window. Remember, you can play the video with changes by pressing the Play button found in the lower left of all the FX dialog boxes.

You can add multiple effects into what's called a plug-in chain, too. Although these chains can't be saved as a group, you can stack FX on FX for unique looks. For example, take any high-motion video and put a Radial Blur and Pinch/Punch together on the moving event. You've got an instant DVD background; you just need to render it out! If there isn't quite enough color, consider adding a color-correction filter and increasing the saturation.

Alternatively, click the Video FX icon found on every event found on the Timeline. This will open the FX dialog as well, showing you all filters found on the event and allowing you to modify the FX on the event. If no FX are on the event, Vegas Movie Studio will prompt you to put FX on the event and offer to show you how.

You can drag and drop additional effects from the window docking area Video FX tab to this dialog to build a chain. Using multiple effects can greatly expand your creative opportunities.

If an event's duration is very short, the button may not display. Either zoom in to reveal the Event FX button or right-click the event and choose Video Event FX from the pop-up menu.

Video Output FX are generally good for global settings such as making an entire video black and white or for creating an old-film effect on the entire video.

To add FX to the entire project, click and drag FX from the Video FX window, and drop it in the Preview window.

The Video Output FX Plug-in dialog displays. Adjust the parameters of the FX described above.

Drag and drop any FX from the Video FX tab of the window docking area directly on to the Preview window, too.

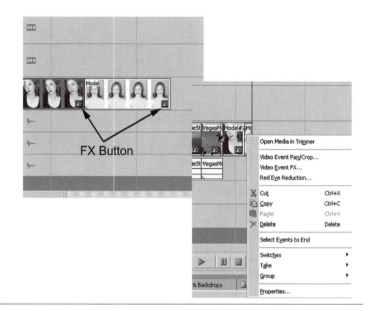

FX Button

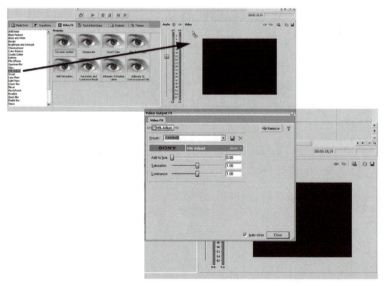

Audio Effects

You can place audio effects on tracks or the project as a whole.

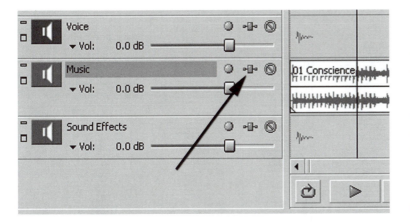

To add Audio FX at the track level, click the Track FX button on an audio track header. All audio events on the track will have the same FX applied.

The Audio Plug-in dialog displays. Notice there is already an EQ in the plug-in chain. To select a plug-in and change its settings, click its corresponding button. The Track EQ shapes the tonal characteristics of sound, just like the EQ that you've likely got on your home stereo or car audio system.

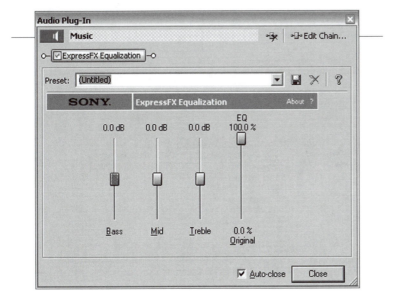

Click the Edit Chain button to add additional effects. A compressor is a good choice for dialog or other non-CD recorded sounds. CD Audio is usually pre-compressed.

The Plug-in Chooser dialog displays. Navigate to the plug-ins you want to apply and click Add to append them to the chain. Here is where you'll select other audio filters. The two most common are dynamic controls and reverbs. Experiment until you find the sound that pleases your ear the most. Dynamic control is also often referred to as compression.

To rearrange a plug-in chain (in the Plug-in Chooser), click, drag, and release the plug-in's button to a new location in the chain. In most cases, Dynamic Control should follow all other filters.

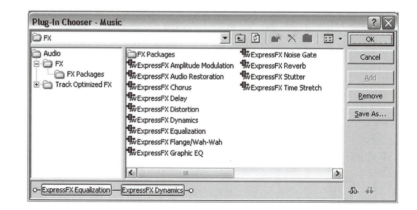

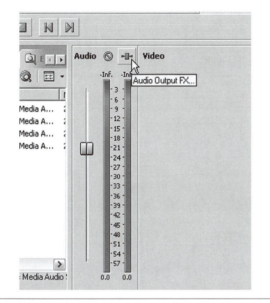

To add audio effects to the master, click the Master FX button found in the Audio control.

The Plug-in Chooser dialog displays. Make selections, add them to the chain by clicking the Add button, and choose OK. In the Master section, Equalizers and Dynamics are generally the best filters to add here if anything is to be added at all. If you find your audio is hitting the red lines or going over, insert a Dynamic control. The Maximize Volume preset is often a good choice.

If an effect has been inserted to the track or the master output, it will be indicated by the FX button turning from gray to green. Any time you see green on an FX button, there is an audio filter inserted on that track or master output.

The dialog box for the chosen plug-in displays. Tweak the parameters as needed.

To bypass FX, remove the check mark adjacent to the plug-in name on its button. To remove it, click the small button with the "X" on it.

Use the bypass button to check the before and after sound of the filter.

Using FX Presets

Consider the Video and Audio FX presets as starting points.

Access video presets from the Video FX window. Drag and drop them as needed.

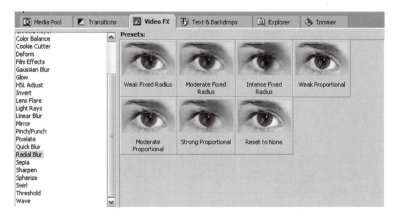

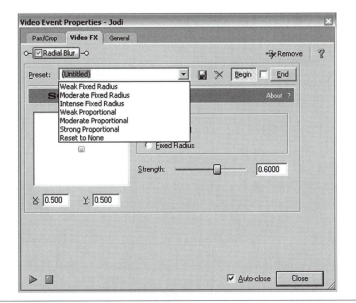

Additionally, after adding Video FX to a track, event, or project, click the corresponding FX button. Choose from the Presets drop-down list.

Audio effects plug-ins also have presets. Click a Track FX button to display the dialog, and choose presets from the drop-down list.

You can save and recall your own FX presets (audio and video). After making changes to the parameters in the dialog box, click the Preset box and type in a unique name. You can recall this at any time.

Remove FX by right-clicking them and selecting Remove.

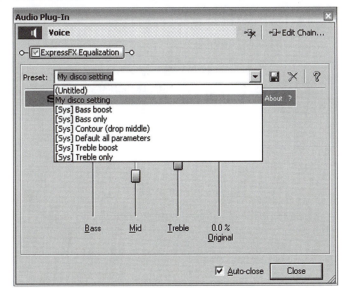

Next, click the Save Preset button.

To delete a preset, call it up from the drop-down list and click the Delete Preset button.

Each FX in a video chain will have its own keyframe control.

Using Keyframes to Change Video FX over Time

"Keyframes" is the name for time-controlling indicators in the filter Timeline. Higher-end professional applications allow multiple keyframes, while most lower-cost applications offer no keyframing. Vegas Movie Studio offers a compromise of a beginning keyframe and an ending keyframe. This means you can modify the parameters of an effect over time.

Add an effect, such as 25 percent Black and White preset, to a video event. The Video Event FX dialog displays.

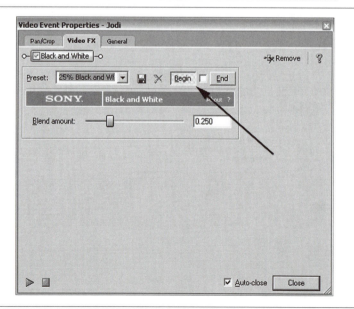

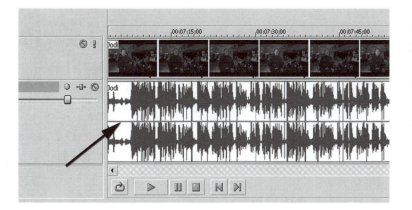

Click the End button and Drag the "Blend amount" slider to 1.000.

Play the event to see it start in color and slowly fade to black and white. Do you notice how the transition is smooth and fluid going from color to black and white?

Use the parameter control to create more interesting effects.

Using Envelopes to Change Audio

Vegas Movie Studio will allow audio to be mixed with what is known as "automation." In other words, Vegas Movie Studio will automatically change volume levels based on envelope controls that you insert.

Click an audio track to select it, and type V to insert a volume envelope. Notice the blue line that runs the entire length of the track. This forms the beginning of the automation process. Some applications call this a "rubber band."

Volume envelopes are blue, and Pan envelopes are Red.

Alternatively, right-click the track and choose Insert/Remove Envelope from the pop-up menu. Envelopes available include Volume and Pan.

Double-click anywhere on the blue line to add a point, or right-click the line and choose Add Point. You can add as many points as needed; there is no limit.

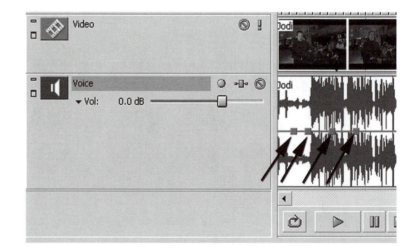

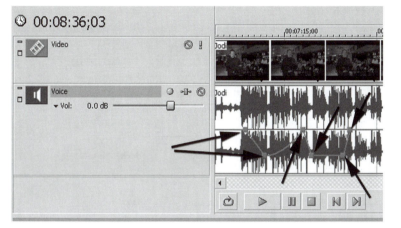

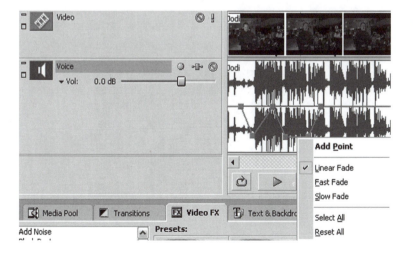

Click and drag the point to a new position to change the envelope.

Right-click a point for additional options including quick preset settings.

Track volume envelopes are relative to the track fader. Zero (0) on the envelope corresponds to the fader setting. Positive envelope values add to the fader; negative envelope values subtract. For example, −12 on the fader with an envelope of −3 equals −15 at that point. Move the envelope to 6, and that equals −6 (−12 + 6) overall.

Right-click the line between points to choose the transition between points. Settings include several fade styles including Linear, Fast, and Slow.

Envelopes can only boost 6dB maximum but can cut to silence (-inf).

Resize, Rotate, and Reverse the Video Image

Vegas Movie Studio provides sophisticated control over the look of every video event. You can crop, rotate, and reverse any video event (including stills and other graphics). This is a great way to create the "Ken Burns" effect seen in so many historical documentaries on television.

Select an event and click its FX button, or right-click it and choose Video Event Pan/Crop from the pop-up menu.

The Event Pan/Crop dialog box displays. The event shows to the right with various controls on the left.

- Show properties—toggles showing and hiding the settings

- Normal Edit Tool—controls the selection box

- Magnify Edit Tool—zooms in and out on the event for fine-tuning selections

- Enable snapping—snaps the selection box to the grid

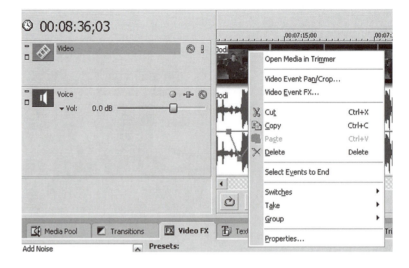

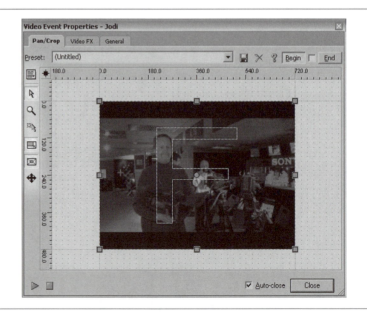

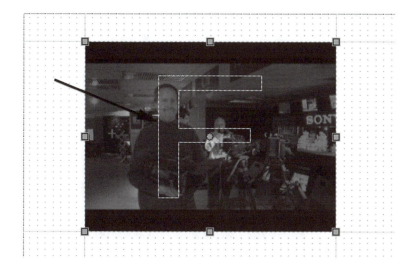

- Lock aspect ratio—resizing maintains the proper project aspect ratio

- Size about center—toggles resizing around the center point or an edge

- Move freely—toggles whether movement is constrained or not

Event Pan/Crop is controllable using the Beginning and End keyframe points, meaning settings can be adjusted as the event plays.

Notice the selection box with handles and its letter F superimposed over the video event. The letter F indicates the focus of the event.

To crop the image, click and drag a handle to the size desired.

Position the selection box within the video frame as needed.

To rotate an event, position the cursor slightly above any edge handle. The cursor changes to a looping arrow.

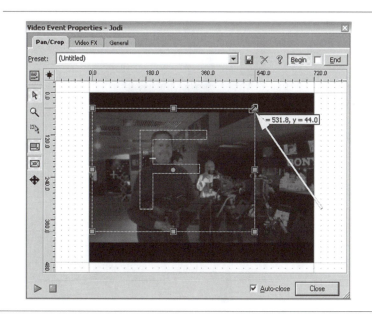

Click and drag in either direction to rotate the video image.

To reverse an event either horizontally or vertically right-click and choose either Flip Horizontal and Flip Vertical. Notice that the letter F is backwards.

Nudge the selection area within the Pan/ Crop dialog using the up, down, left, and right arrow keys.

You can also enter values directly into the Properties settings.

Picture-in-Picture Effects

The alternative to cropping an event is to make the whole event (or part of an event) smaller. This technique allows having more that one event displayed.

Vegas Movie Studio will allow you to do picture-in-picture video. Using Event Pan/Crop as discussed above, enter larger numbers in the size box to "shrink" the image. For example, 1440 makes the DV video one-quarter size. Position the smaller event as needed.

Use Begin/End keyframes to animate the effect. You can have the video move across the screen and change size at the same time.

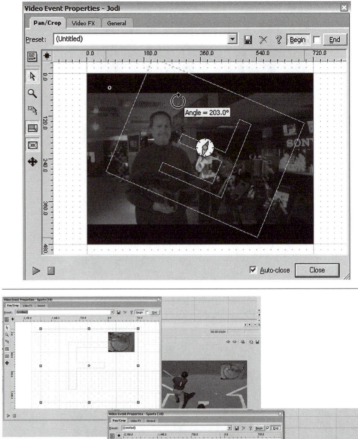

Notice the Pn'P moved to the left!

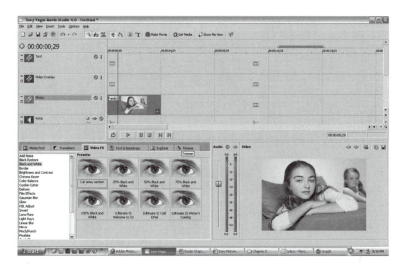

This example uses three tracks, each with separate video events. The top two clips were resized (320×240) and positioned using Track Motion. The third clip shows through underneath, allowing you to see three layers of video at the same time.

If you want to layer a title over the three layers, you'll need to render the three layers as a new file, import the new file to the Timeline as a finished video selection, and then create titles over top of the new file.

Set the default duration of stills using Options> Preferences> Editing tab and enter a value for "New still image length (seconds)."

Adding Motion to Stills

Another use of Event Pan/Crop is to emulate the popular "Burns Brothers" documentary look of zooming and panning on photos. This used to be done with tracking cameras and expensive hardware, but now you can do this with family photos and create all kinds of fun and interesting effects.

Drag and drop a still photo on the Timeline.

Select it and click the FX button, or right-click the event and choose the Event Pan/Crop option in the menu.

Animate with pan, zoom, and rotation to give the illusion of movement to still images.

You can have a beginning size and position and an ending size and position. The differences (if any) between the beginning and ending is what will animate the photo.

Click an edge handle of the selection box and drag in, or crop the image so that it is smaller. Remember, shrinking the focus box will enlarge the image in the Preview window, and enlarging the focus box will reduce the image in the Preview window.

Play the Timeline to see the picture zoom. If it's animated to your satisfaction, you can move on to the next image.

If the photo doesn't match the aspect ratio of your project, black bands may appear. You may leave them in place or you can quickly crop the picture to fill the screen.

If a picture is sideways, rotate the image using Event Pan/Crop to the proper perspective.

If you'd like to rotate the image to make it more interesting, or to create a "Dutch Tilt," then use the rotation tool in the Pan/Crop tool to create the rotation.

Right-click the still in the Event Pan/Crop dialog and choose Match Output Aspect to automatically adjust to fit. Make any necessary adjustments by using the handles.

Sometimes adding motion to photos as described can introduce some jitter, or interlace flicker, when the project plays on TV.

It's a good idea to avoid very high-resolution pictures as they are more prone to interlace issues. Occasionally, adding a slight .002 blur to very high-resolution images will fix this jitter. Drag and drop the Quick Blur effect from the Video FX tab of the FX window.

Set the Amount to 0.002. You might want to save this setting as a preset if you intend on doing several still images.

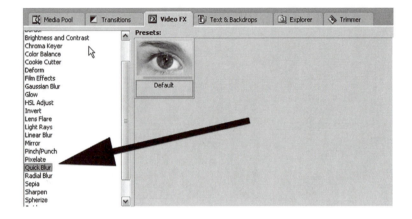

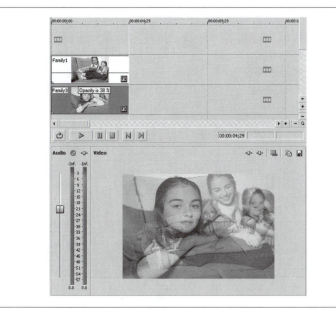

Level Opacity Superimposition

You can combine multiple video events using opacity. If you make a top event semi-transparent, the next track below shows through. The two tracks superimpose like a dissolve that reaches halfway but never finishes. As mentioned before, this is known as compositing.

Start with two events on two separate video tracks.

Adjust any event's opacity level by hovering near the top of the event until the icon changes to a pointing hand. Click and drag down to reduce opacity (increase transparency). In this particular case, lower the opacity of the top event by half. Notice that the image below shows through.

Masking

Use masks as overlays to create fun and exciting effects. A mask is an image that has transparency so that other video layers can show through. For example, in this image you can see a city skyline in the front and a second image in the back.

Create masks in your favorite image editing software. You can download the mask seen in this image from the VASST site.

Place an event on the video track.

Using your photo editing software, remove areas of the image you'd like to be transparent. Remember that digital video uses non-square pixels, so you'll either need to use image sizes of 655×480 or 1310×960, or plan on using Pan/Crop to correctly display the aspect ratio.

Save this file as a PNG or TGA for best results. You will not be able to use TIF files in Vegas Movie Studio unless you install the QuickTime application from the www.quicktime.com site.

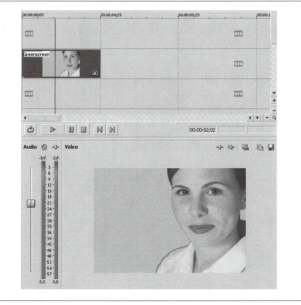

Chromakey Compositing

Chromakey (color mask) is a way to remove a specific color and replace it with something else. For example, shoot a subject in front of a green-screen and replace the green with a suitable background, such as a weather map. You can emulate this special effect, too. In television news, blue is often used as a background color, but for digital video, green is best.

First, shoot your subject against a well-lit green background. I recommend the Photoflex FlexDrop 2 portable background. It comes green on one side and blue on the reverse, so it's very versatile.

Capture the footage and drop it on the Timeline. Place the background footage on the Timeline, one track lower. If you download the Vegas Movie Studio package from www.vasst.com, you'll find this image available as a greenscreen demonstration.

Switch to the Video FX tab in the window docking area, navigate to the Chroma Keyer FX, and choose the Green Screen preset.

Drag and drop the FX on the event with the subject against the green-screen.

The Chroma Keyer dialog displays.

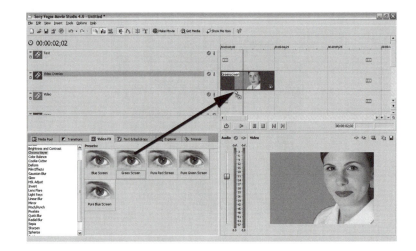

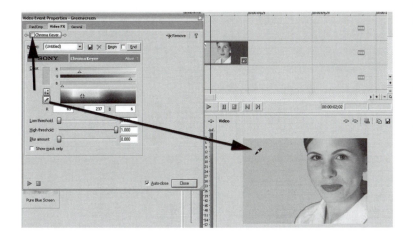

Turn off the effect for a moment by unchecking the box inside the effect's button. Click the Pick Color from Screen tool (the eyedropper).

Click and drag it over the green portion in the Preview window. This sets the key color to the exact shade of green from your footage.

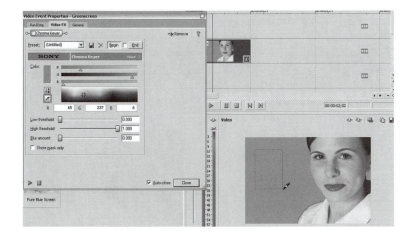

Turn the chroma key effect back on. The composite should look better. You'll probably need to adjust the Threshold controls for better matching of the image to the background.

For a cool "ghosting" effect, keep Show Mask Only checked and adjust for the look.

For further fine-tuning, click the Show Mask Only checkbox. It's much easier to adjust the mask in black and white, simply because the human eye is a lot more sensitive to contrast in light than it is to changes in color. Use the Show Mask Only to convert the mask to black and white. You want to see solid black in the areas to be cut out and solid white in the areas that will remain.

The Preview window shows only the mask generated by the effect.

Use the Low threshold and High threshold sliders to adjust the effect until the subject is pure white and the surrounding greenscreen area is deep black.

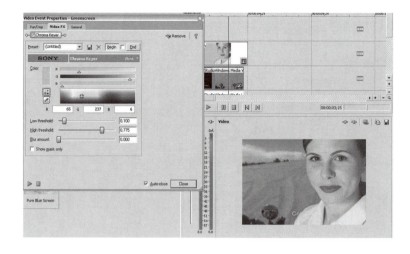

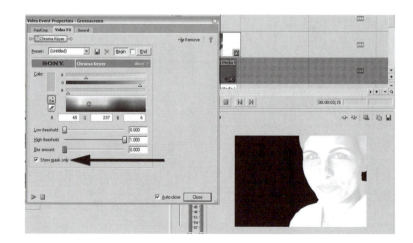

Remove the check from the Show Mask Only checkbox, and the composite should look perfect.

Green is the best key color to use for digital video. Make sure you light the greenscreen evenly (avoid shadows and hot spots). Keep the subject's shadow off the screen, and prevent the green light from spilling on the subject. Also, match the lighting of the replacement background.

Chapter 6

Titling Tools and Text Techniques

You can't have a video project without titles. Titles in Vegas Movie Studio can be very creative and fun, and the more interesting your titles are, the more interested your audience will remain.

Basic Titles

If you draw a time selection before adding a title, its duration will be the selected length.

Vegas Movie Studio provides several built-in media generators: colors, gradients, credit rolls, and text. Switch to the Media Generators tab in the window docking area and scroll through the options. Notice that there are several text styles available.

To insert a title on a video track, select Text from the Text and Backdrops pane, and drag and drop Default Text to the Timeline. Set the default duration in Options>Preferences>Editing tab. Of course, you can extend the title as needed.

By default, text events are set to 10 seconds. However, you can extend them as long as you'd like by dragging out the title, or you can use the text length dialog box.

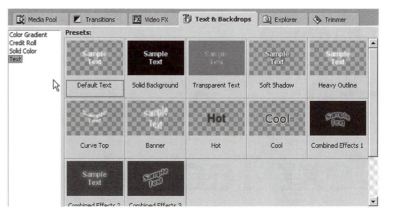

Alternatively, select a track and then right-click in the Timeline and choose Insert Text Media from the pop-up menu.

The Video Media Generator: Sony Text dialog box displays. There are four tabs.

- Edit—picks the font, size, bold, italics, and left, center, right justification. It's also where you type the text. You can mix and match fonts, sizes, and so forth.

- Placement—positions the text on the screen. Simply click and drag the title into position. Click the drop-down box and choose from the list for preset locations.

Projects destined for TV playback must use legal colors. Keep color values between 16 and 235 (defaults range between 0 and 255).

- Properties—adjusts text and background colors along with tracking, leading, and scaling. These settings are global for the entire text event. They apply to *all* text entered via the Edit tab.

- Effects—chooses outline, shadow, and deformation options. These, too, are global effects for all text entered in this event.

Note that the text on the Timeline has a grayscale checkerboard pattern. This indicates alpha channel information; the text has a transparent background.

If you place the text on the text track with video on the track beneath it, the title automatically superimposes over the video. Although the text track is labeled as such, you can put text on any track you want to.

Create titles in other graphics programs and save to the PNG format to retain their alpha channel information on the Timeline. Create them at 655x480 for best results.

To edit text already on the Timeline, click the text event's FX button. Notice that when the dialog opens, there are three other tabs in the Text dialog box.

Text are events and can therefore be treated with Pan/Crop, FX, and transitions just as any other event. This is how you can sweeten text events to make them fly into the picture, out of the picture, or have changing colors or special FX just like you can do with video. All video FX can be applied to text for interesting looks.

For unique looks, consider stacking two text tracks with different settings on each other for creative stylings.

For the best legibility, use sans serif fonts, such as Arial and Impact, and keep them big and bold. Avoid fonts that have fine lines and that are thin.

Fonts with small serifs can be hard to read and may also look jittery because of video interlacing.

Play It Safe

If your project will play on a standard TV, it's crucial to keep titles away from the edges. TVs often crop, or cut off, the extreme edges. To avoid this, place titles inside an area that is 10 to 20 percent in from the screen edge.

On the Placement tab of the Text dialog box, there is a red border that indicates the title safe area as set by the adjacent Safe Zone drop-down list.

If your project will play only on a computer, you may ignore title-safe guidelines.

This area indicates the safe area for titles. If your titles stray outside the red area, you likely will see your title lettering going off screen in your production.

Although the title might not be off the screen in the Preview window, when it shows on a standard television, it likely will be off screen or at least partially obscured by the television's side bezels.

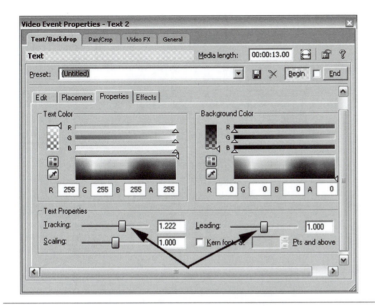

A popular look is to have text either spread out or compressed slightly. It's a subtle (or not so subtle effect) that adds some motion to an otherwise static shot. You can achieve this with the Beginning/End keyframe option while using the Tracking option found in the Text Properties tab.

Preview the text event and watch how it either expands or contracts as it plays.

Even though Vegas Movie Studio doesn't offer multiple keyframes, you can make it act as though it does. Split an event into three pieces, and in the begin keyframe of the first event, set a behavior. In the end keyframe, set the behavior to Off. In the middle event, leave it with no keyframed behaviors. In the end event, begin the event with no changes, but end with a new action. This will create the illusion of moving keyframes. You can see this effect in the downloaded Vegas Movie Studio project.

Roll the Credits

Click the Text and Backdrops tab in the window docking area and select Credit Roll in the left pane. Drag the Scrolling on Transparent preset to the Timeline.

The Video Media Generator: Sony Credit Roll dialog box displays. Enter text in the left pane. Change properties on the right.

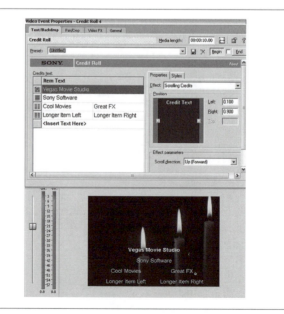

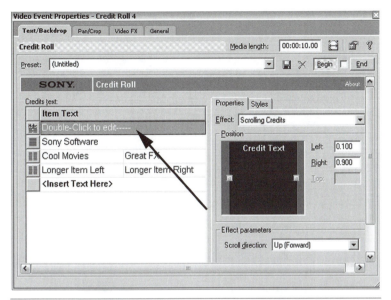

In place already are sample text and styles. Double-click to edit them. To add a line, double-click Insert Text Here and type.

Click the Style Selection to apply a style to the line.

Double-click any slider to return it to its default value.

Under Properties, choose the effect, Scrolling Credit or Timed Sequence, from the drop-down list.

For Scrolling Credits, adjust the Position and Scroll Direction.

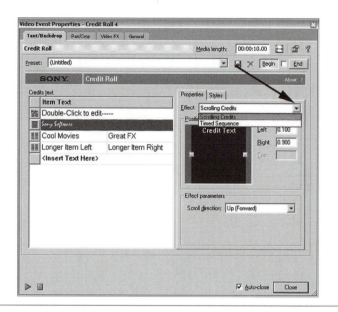

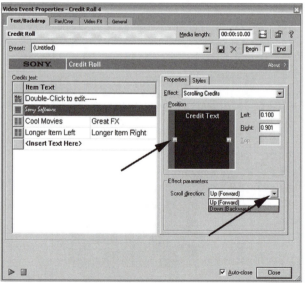

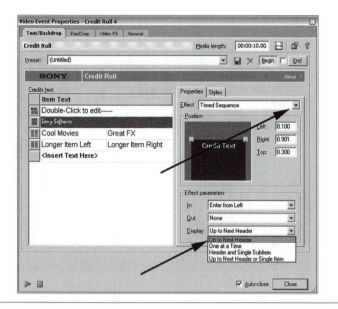

For Timed Sequence, adjust the position and effects parameters.

- In—choose an entry transition

- Out—choose an exit transition

- Display—indicate how the text appears on screen

Click the Styles tab to change the style look. Choose a Style Name from the drop-down list to change its parameters.

You can create your credit rolls in Microsoft Excel and copy and paste them to the Credit Roll dialog.

When complete, preview the credits.

The Star Wars look

Create a credit roll as described above. Switch to the Video FX tab in the window docking area and navigate to the Deform plug-in. Hold Shift and drag the Squeeze Top preset and drop it on the credit roll event.

In the Perspective box, hover over the Y, click, and drag up to position the text. Eyeball the Preview window as you adjust. Also, make sure your keyframe is the first and only keyframe. Close the dialog.

Preview your very recognizable credit roll. Fanfare anyone?

Create a Lower-Third Graphic in Vegas Movie Studio

Titles that extend across the bottom of the screen, called lower-thirds, are useful to convey names, locations, and other information. Sometimes these are called name boards.

Create a new project and place the main video on the video track.

Click the Text and Backdrops tab, select color gradient, and then Fancy Wooden Board to the Overlay track on the Timeline.

The Video Media Generator: Sony Color Gradient dialog displays. Adjust the look to taste and close the dialog.

Double-click the color gradient to create a time selection. Right-click in the Text track above and choose Insert Text Media to add a title.

In the text dialog, type and resize the text using the Edit tab.

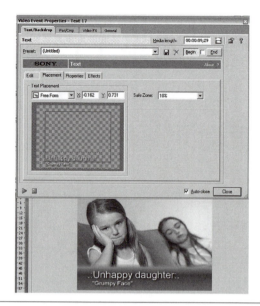

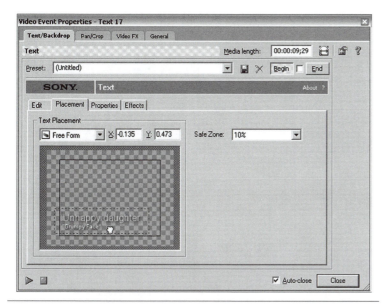

Click the Placement tab and drag the title into position using the Preview window to check the progress. When finished, close the dialog.

Add a Fade-In to the Lower-Third Graphic

Select Linear Wipe from the Transitions tab and drag the Left-Right, Soft Edge preset to the fade-in. Add a simple fade-out to the end of the event.

Shorten the title event and move it to the right slightly so it starts later. Add a fade-in and fade-out.

Preview the result. The lower-third graphic wipes in, the title fades in over the top, then they fade out together.

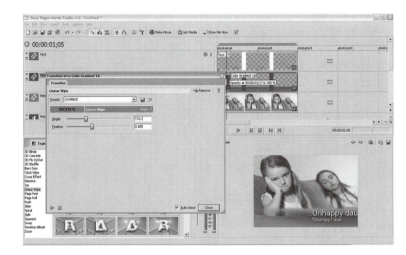

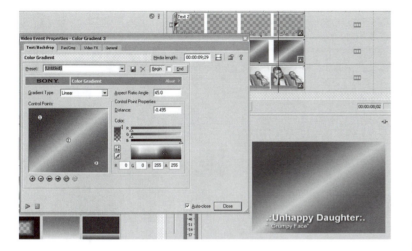

Creating a Different Type of Lower-Third

Click the Text and Colors tab, select color gradient, and then drag the Linear Red, Green, and Blue preset to track two on the Timeline.

The Video Event Properties—Color Gradient dialog displays. Adjust the look to taste.

Switch to the Pan/Crop tab. Turn off the Lock Aspect Ratio button. Position the gradient using these settings as a starting point: Size: 575✕275 and Center 300✕22.

Place a title over the lower-third as described in the previous section.

Add a "Bug"

TV and videos often use graphics in the lower-right corner to brand their content. These icons and logos are called bugs.

Create a video track and make it the
first track. This way no matter what
else happens on your other video
tracks, the bug is always there. Place
the bug on this track and extend its
duration for the project length.

Click the FX button to display the
Pan/Crop dialog. Make sure the Lock
Aspect ration button is engaged. Then,
resize the Pan/Crop area by clicking
and dragging a corner of the box. Remember, to make the bug smaller, you
need to enlarge the Pan/Crop window.

Position in the lower right (mind the
title-safe boundaries). Right-click
inside the Pan/Crop dialog if you need
to zoom out, or use your mouse wheel
if you have one.

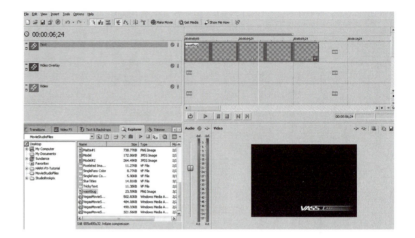

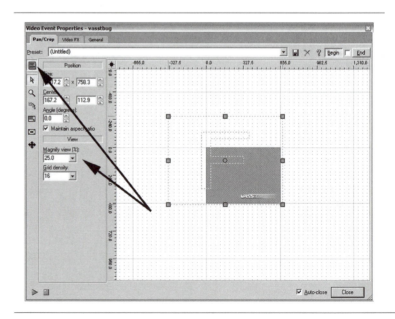

Chapter 7

Sound Off!

Vegas Movie Studio provides wide-ranging tools for making your video look great. However, unlike many other NLEs where audio is an afterthought, Sony's audio approach fully integrates with the video portion. Vegas Movie Studio provides excellent audio tools that will allow you to record your own voice-over, sweeten CD tracks, and improve your video audio.

Audio is 70 percent of what the viewer "sees" in your program. Don't believe us? Turn on your favorite movie and turn off the sound. Not quite the same, is it? You can get by with less-than-perfect video, but audio is what will help keep focus on your project. Spend the time working to get your audio as clear and present as possible, and you'll be surprised at how much more your video will be appreciated.

Sound Messages

Most of the tips and techniques explained so far apply to audio. Like video, audio is just another event on the Timeline. When it comes to editing, trimming, moving, crossfading, and arranging, treat audio just like video. In fact, Vegas Movie Studio provides audio tools that are very similar to the video tools, which helps you in turn by not having to learn two different workflows as you would with most applications.

One of the great features of both programs is the ability to watch the video as you record sound. This makes recording in sync with the picture a snap.

Audio doesn't follow the top-down motif as video. All audio is available when on the Timeline, and you have several methods for controlling the way that the audio events blend with each other:

- Track levels for the overall level of each track.

- Mute and Solo buttons.

- Audio event attack, sustain, release (ASR) envelope for fading in (A), main level (R), and fading out (S). Move to the top of the audio event and drag the little pointing finger down. Move to either edge of the audio event (cursor changes to a pie shape) and drag for fades. Right-click for fade choices.

- Track volume (and pan) envelope on a track to automate level over time. Vegas includes automation recording, too.

- Master bus fader for overall project level.

Many of these were discussed earlier in the book; others will be featured here.

Audio for Video Secrets

Audiences will put up with "bad" video, but *never* poor sound. Poor audio ruins the experience and immediately screams "amateur"! Memorable soundtracks have the power to inform, entertain, and elicit the desired emotional response. Thankfully, audio is often the easiest and cheapest way to make your video production look better and deliver the message more effectively.

Following are some basic guidelines.

- Focus on capturing voice in production. Dialog carries the most important message. Other sounds can be added in post-production.

- The typical built-in camcorder microphone is good for one thing: picking up the noise of the camera. Use a separate, directional microphone whenever possible.

- The best mic technique is to point the mic at the source of the sound you want and get as close as possible to it. No quality of mic can substitute for being close to your subject.

- Consider using clip-on lavaliere mics for interviews. Hide them on sets to capture actors.

- Use a directional mic on a fishpole boom for dramatic scenes or when a lav won't work.

- Always capture some presence or room tone at every location. Use it in post to smooth voice edits. (Just let the camera roll while there is no other sound in the room, recording the sound of the "air" in the room.)

- Layer your soundscape by adding sound effects, background sounds, and music in post-production.

- Keep sound "families" on their own tracks. Don't mix dialog and sound effects on the same track. Use different tracks and checkerboard sounds across the Timeline.

- Balance the elements in a mix to make speech intelligibility the number-one priority.

- Find a place for everything in the mix. Use contrast and dynamics, and fill the frequency spectrum.

Prepare to Record

To get started recording, hook up an audio source. For example, to record a voice-over (VO), connect the mic to the soundcard. If using an external mic preamp or a mixer, connect the mic to the preamp or mixer first and then its line inputs to the soundcard. Refer to the instructions that came with your soundcard or mixer for details about hooking up audio sources.

Set levels at the preamp or mixer and also using any software that controls the soundcard. For example, access the standard Windows soundcard controls from Start>Control Panel> Sounds and Audio Devices. If there is a speaker icon in the Taskbar, click it to access the same tools.

Click the advanced tab to show the Windows volume control. The default shows the playback levels of the various sound devices connected to your computer system.

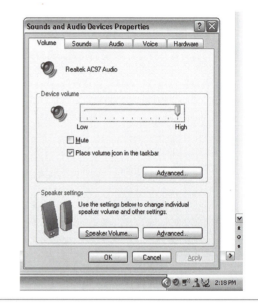

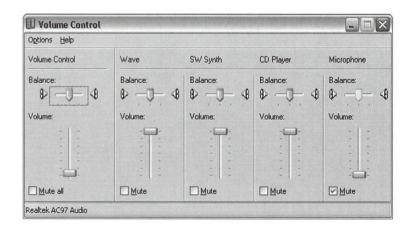

Click Options>Properties to switch to the soundcard's recording settings.

Select the Recording button and click OK.

Choose the appropriate input device. In this example, click the checkbox under CD Player and use the slider to adjust the level. Alternately, select microphone and adjust the level accordingly. Under the Advanced tab are additional microphone settings.

Next, setup a folder to hold your recording. Setup the record folder using File>Project Properties>Folders>Media Folder.

Recording Audio

Sound is captured along with the video during the video capture step. However, sometimes you need to record additional parts.

Extracting audio from a CD is explained earlier in this book.

- Dialog (production dialog and voice-over)

- Sound effects (hard effects and backgrounds)

- Foley (footsteps, clothing, and props)

- Music

When choosing music for your production, ask these questions: What emotional response do you desire? What style is appropriate? Where will you use music specifically? Is the music the driving force behind the scene, or is there dialog over the music?

While you may record many of these elements yourself, some may come from outside resources. You can find some resources by clicking the Get Media button.

Sound effects libraries:

- The Hollywood Edge, www.hollywood-edge.com

- Sonomic, www.sonomic.com

- SoundDogs.com, www.sounddogs.com

- Sound Effects Library.com, www.sound-effects-library.com

Production music libraries:

- Digital Juice, www.digitaljuice.com

- Fresh Music, www.freshmusic.com

- Killer Tracks, www.killertracks.com

- Music Bakery, www.musicbakery.com

- Omnimusic, www.omnimusic.com

- VideoHelper, www.videohelper.com

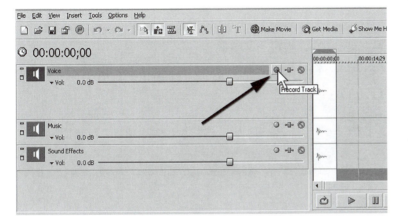

Select the Voice Track and locate the Arm for Record button. Do not click it until you are ready to start recording.

When you click Record, the application will begin recording immediately. Pay close attention to levels; you do not want the output to trigger the "over" indicator at any time. Let the audio just barely move into the red zone.

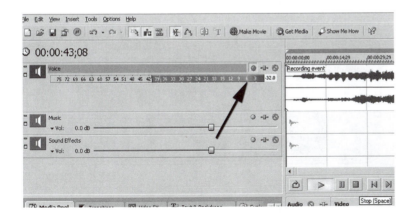

Notice the meters displaying in the track. Keep your recording levels between –18 and –3 for the best results. The Volume slider controls only the playback volume of the track, not the record level. Use the Microsoft mixer or your soundcard controls to set levels.

Never let your audio recording exceed zero on the meters, or it will sound distorted.

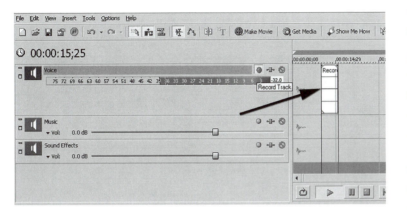

Click the record button or use the Ctrl+R shortcut. Vegas begins recording on the voice track at the cursor position.

When recording is complete, click Stop or press Esc, and the Recorded Files dialog displays. Choose from the options accordingly. You can save the audio to a folder, or delete the audio you've just recorded. Notice that the file is named with the same name as the voice track. If you wish, double-click the voice track name dialog and give the voice track a new name prior to recording. The new name will be part of the filename.

You may also record voice or other audio onto the remaining two audio tracks.

Cleaning Up Production Dialog

Getting good sound on location is difficult, at best. While you should strive to get the best recordings possible up front, there are a few fixes available.

Whether it's an interview or a dramatic scene, one common mistake picture editors make is always cutting the audio and video in the same place. This is a simple procedure: position the cursor and press S to cut both audio and video. The problem is that audio often doesn't blend smoothly from shot to shot. Tying it to an abrupt visual statement only compounds the audio jump.

Good dialog editors overcome this problem by either cutting just before or after the picture cut, or by using audio crossfades, or both. From a workflow standpoint, you'll probably want to cut the audio and video at the same time first. Then, go back and smooth the dialog later after the visuals are complete.

Called the J edit, it involves cutting the dialog when the person finishes speaking before the picture cuts to someone else. This brings in the next shot's audio earlier. Select the corresponding audio event, right-click it, and choose Group> Remove From to ungroup the audio from its video, or use the shortcut U.

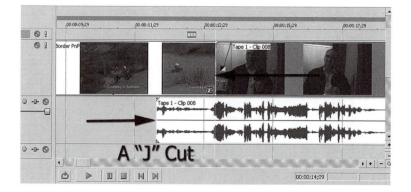

Shorten the event, being careful not to cut off any words or parts of words.

Ungroup the adjacent audio event and extend to fill the gap. A short overlap can further smooth the dialog.

Checkerboarding the voice events on adjacent tracks can make dialog smoothing easier.

To make an L cut, extend the previous cut's sound until the next person starts talking. The person's speech covers up the edit well. Select the second sound event and ungroup it from its video. Shorten it until the dialog starts. Listen carefully as you might cut off a breath.

Select the first sound event, ungroup it, and drag it out to fill the gap. Crossfades are optional.

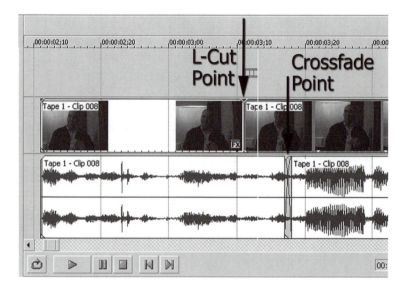

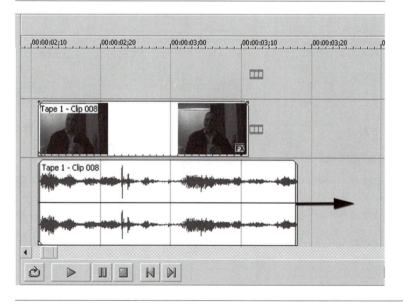

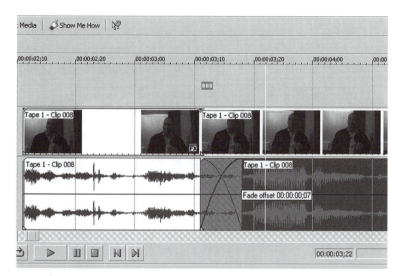

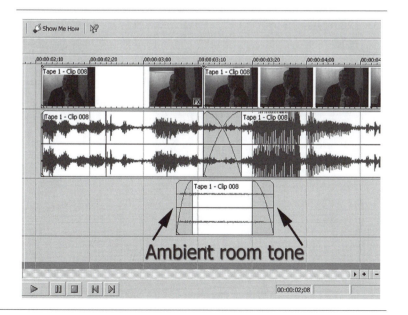

Ambient room tone

Or simply use crossfades on the tracks to smooth the dialog.

Another trick is to use room tone or presence recorded on location to fill in the gaps and further smooth the dialog edits. The idea is to have a smooth sound, free of annoying sound jumps. Previously we mentioned recording some of the room's "air" so that you'll have it for edits. This is where you'll use the "air" of the room.

More often than not, steady noise or background sounds cover up edits best. The ear and brain are rather adept at tuning out the background noise and focusing on what's being said. It's when the presence jumps from shot to shot that draws attention to the problem and ruins the illusion. For example, you have wind noise in some dialog, but not all. Add wind noise recorded on location under the dialog during the whole sequence.

Equalization affects the tonal balance of sounds. Vegas Movie Studio includes the Track EQ plug-in by default on every audio channel. I recommend you replace it with the Express FX Graphic EQ to make the below settings.

Try these general settings when working with production dialog.

- Roll off the extreme lows from 80Hz down to get rid of rumble and subsonic noise.

- Add a 2–4dB bump at 113Hz to add warmth to male voice, 320Hz for female.

- Add 2–4dB at 1.8kHz, or 3.6kHz, or both, for speech intelligibility. This may bring out excessive "ess" sounds, called sibilance.

- Add 2–4dB in the 7.2kHz area to add some sparkle to a dull recording.

- Drop the muddy midrange by 2–4dB in the 500–800Hz range.

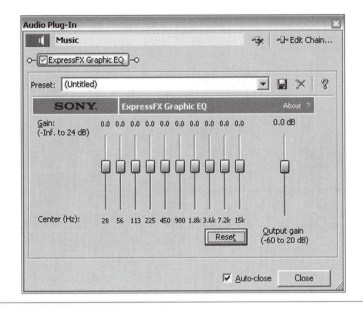

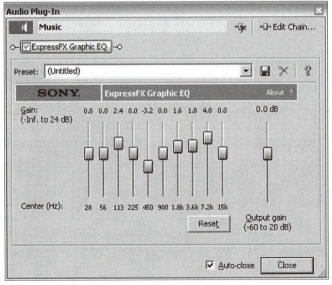

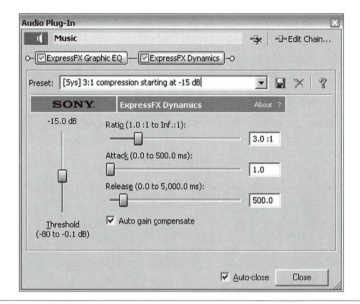

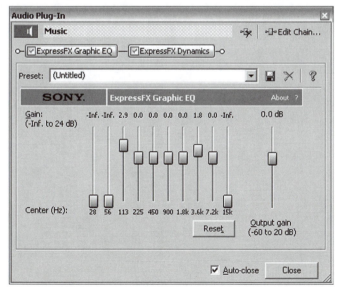

You should consider adding Track Dynamics and choose the 3:1 compression starting at –15 dB Preset to further smooth the dialog level.

Eliminating Noise

If your recording has too much room and not enough speech (caused by having the mic too far away in a large room), you may be able to fix it somewhat. (It'll never be perfect, though.)

Add the Graphic EQ to the offending track and use these settings

- Pull the 28Hz and 56Hz sliders all the way off or down. Do the same with the 15kHz slider as well.

- For a male voice, raise the 113 slider by 3dB or so, and raise the 3.6kHz slider by about the same amount. For a female voice, raise the 225Hz slider by 3dB and set the 3.6kHz slider to the same amount of increase.

You may need to adjust other frequencies according to what you're hearing through your monitor speakers. If necessary, add another instance of the EQ to the chain by pressing the FX button, choosing the Graphic EQ from the FX dialog, and clicking "Add." Use multiple EQs only if you have a frequency range that is very troublesome.

Got some hum on your recording? Add the Graphic EQ to the humming Track FX chain. You'll need to stack a couple of these on. Take the 56Hz slider all the way down. Do the same on another instance, while pulling the 113Hz slider all the way down on one instance. This won't completely eliminate the noise, but it will help. You can also open the audio file in Sound Forge Audio Studio and use the EQ there if you wish. (It's the same EQ in both applications).

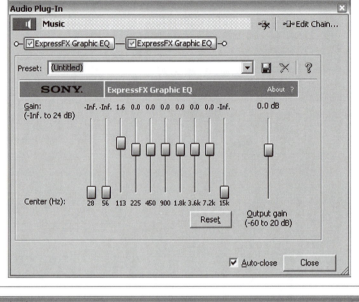

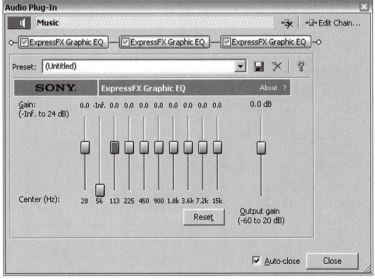

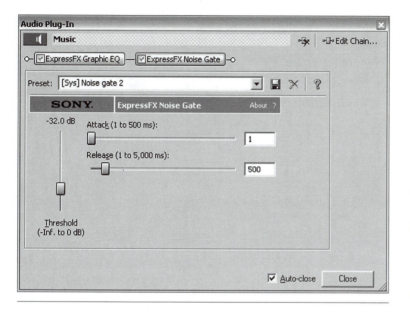

Another way to eliminate noise on a track is via the Express FX Track Noise Gate. However, this device works like a switch, essentially turning off the track to eliminate the noise when there is no dialog and turning it back on when the dialog plays. The noise will still be under the dialog but should be masked by the speech. Therefore, the constant cutting in and out of the noise may make the track sound worse, not better. Let your ears determine what sounds best.

To turn off noise on a track, use the Express FX Noise Gate. Play the track and set the Threshold so the noise goes away. Higher settings mean more noise gets cut off, but be careful not to chop of starts and ends of words.

By far the best way to eliminate noise is to use the Express FX Audio Restoration plug-in. It's got tools to eliminate clicks, crackles, and pops in your audio.

Sound Mangling

As fun as many Video FX are, there are also some unique audio effects available.

Make a voice sound as if it's coming from a telephone by pulling all frequencies down except for the 1.8kHz slider. Leave it set to 0, or even increase its level by a little bit.

Make alien and otherworldly sounds by applying the Express FX Flange/Wah-Wah plug-in to the track. Go through the various presets until you find the sound you want.

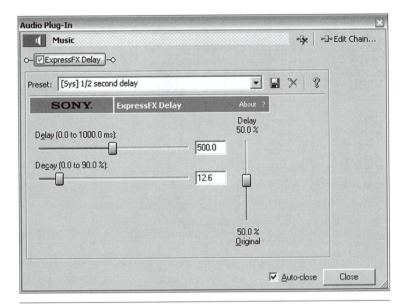

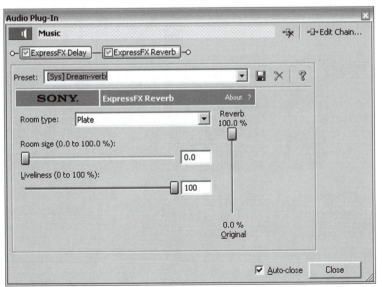

Add distinct repeats to a track using the Express Delay plug-in. Try the ½ Second preset and engage the Decays (Feedback) by moving the slider to 30.0.

Create a variety of rooms in which to place your sounds using the Reverb plug-in. Again, presets can get you started. Adjust to your specific taste.

You can also save audio FX chains in Vegas Movie Studio. If you have multiple FX on an audio file, click the FX button on the audio track header, and choose Save As in the dialog. This will allow you to save the sequence of FX and their parameter values as a single group of FX to be recalled at any time.

Integration with Sound Forge Audio Studio

For more extensive audio editing chores, Vegas Movie Studio integrates with Sound Forge Audio Studio. Right-click an audio event and choose Open Copy in Sound Editor. It's better to open a copy rather than the original event, so that you're only working with a copy instead of affecting the original file.

Use the tools in Sound Forge and then save the file.

Switch to Vegas, and the fixed file shows up as a take. The original file remains, too.

You'll be able to switch between takes by highlighting the audio file and pressing the T key. This will allow you to go back and forth between the processed file and the original file. You can also right-click the audio, and in the Takes dialog, specify which audio you'd like to listen to.

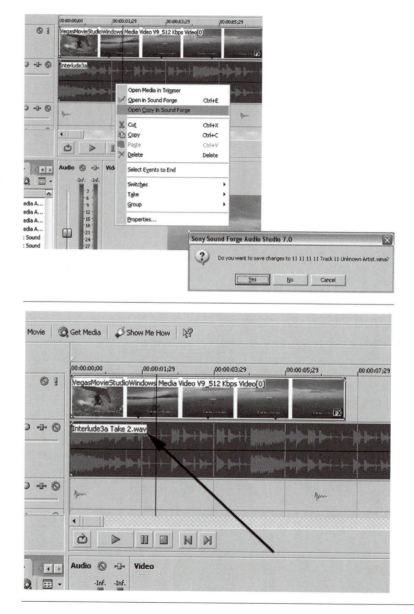

Chapter 8

Getting Creative with Techniques

Are you looking for some eye candy to entertain, motivate, and inform your audiences? This grab bag of techniques should get your creative energy flowing.

Fast, Slow, Reverse, Strobe, and Ghost

Hold Ctrl and click and drag a video file to the upper track to quickly make a copy.

Remember to use Ctrl+dragging/trimming events to slow down or speed up video. However, there is one other method. Right-click an event and choose Properties. Adjust the Playback rate. Higher numbers speed up and lower numbers slow down the video.

One sweet technique is to duplicate a video event on an upper track, and change the playback speed of the event on the upper track.

Adjust the opacity (40 to 60 percent) of the upper event to blend. This can create a dreamy quality to the video. For a different look, apply the Black and White FX to the bottom track, too. Notice in this illustration that there are now two hang gliders.

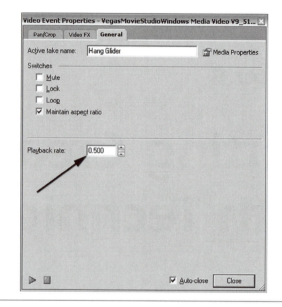

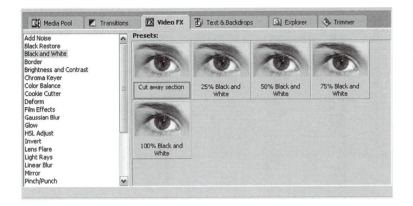

Black and White and Old Film Looks

Select the Video FX tab in the window docking area and navigate to Black and White. Drag and drop one of the presets to a video track or event for the grayscale look.

The Sepia Video FX simulates old photos, video, home movies, or a nostalgic look.

For an old film look, use the Film Effects Video FX. Place the effect on either an event or the entire project. Adjust the properties for the effect you want.

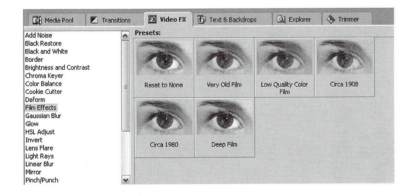

Add the Glow FX preset White Soft Glow and reduce Intensity to 1.8 for a unique spin on the old movie theme. Glow can impart a dreamlike, flashback, or romantic look, too.

Unique Color and Shape effects

The Threshold Video FX yields a posterized look. Combine it with the Black and White filter for more creative options.

Create a Flash transition to simulate taking pictures. Add the appropriate sound effect to complete the illusion. Create the effect by dropping a very short (one frame) event of white or almost white generated media on the Overlay track above your edit point.

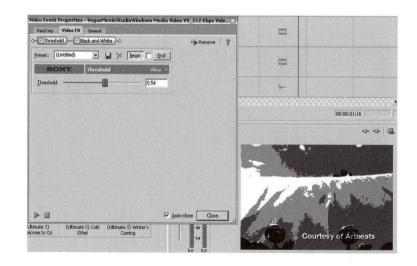

Courtesy of Artbeats

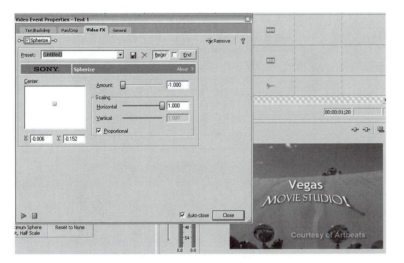

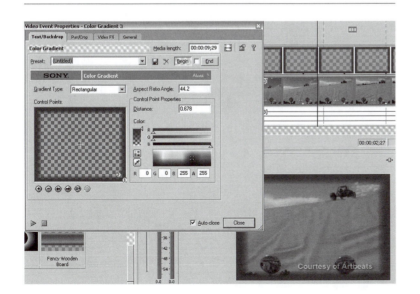

Distort the video using Pinch/Punch, Spherize, Swirl, or Wave. Drag the filter to the track or event and go through the presets for some instant effects. Animate these effects using the Begin/End for unique ideas.

These unusual effects are ideal for dressing up titles and simulating 3D looks.

Create two different title events and add the Wave video FX to both.

This is another means of creating a cool and effective title.

Need some inspiration? Watch *Entertainment Tonight*, *Access Hollywood*, or any music video channel. Emulate what you see with your projects.

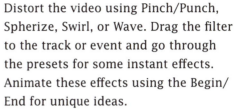

Borders, Widescreen, and Letterboxing

Place a border around the video by dragging the Translucent Blue Border preset to a video event or track. Adjust the color and opacity of the border as needed. Use Pan/Crop in Vegas Movie Studio to create a picture-in-picture (PIP) look discussed earlier in this book. You'll need to duplicate the size of the translucent border on the overlay track.

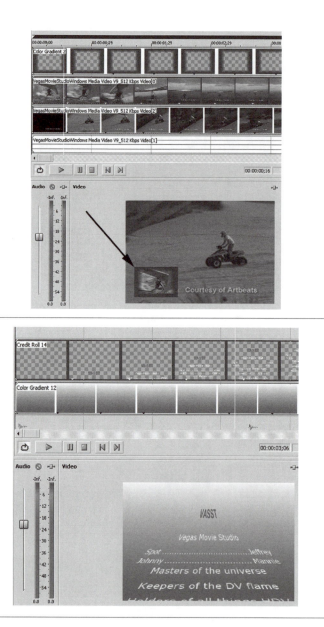

One trick to this is to copy the translucent border from the upper track, and then right-click the video file to be used as picture-in-picture, and drag it to the lower translucent blue movie border, and select Add as Takes. Now the motion and size of the video file match the translucent blue border.

Use Event Pan/Crop to match the widescreen aspect ratio.

Simulate 3D looks using the Deform Video FX. Drop the Deform plug-in on the event. Start with the Squeeze Left preset and adjust the Squeeze Left slider to 0.300 for a simulated look. Work with the Shear sliders (try –0.3H and 0.25V) to perfect the effect.

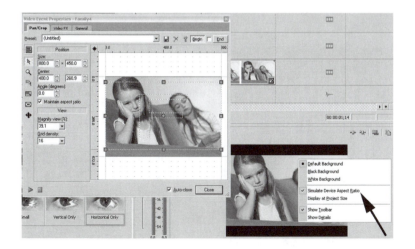

Use the W key to rewind your project to the beginning point.

Turn your project into the 16×9 widescreen format. Click File>Project Properties and choose and the NTSC DV Widescreen template from the drop-down list.

Right-click the Preview window and choose Simulate Device Aspect Ratio to get an accurate view of the widescreen format.

Another neat trick with Vegas Movie Studio is that you can double-click anywhere in the Preview window to alternate between the small resolution display and full size display. This is handy when checking critical details.

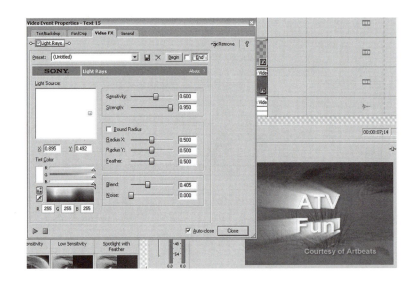

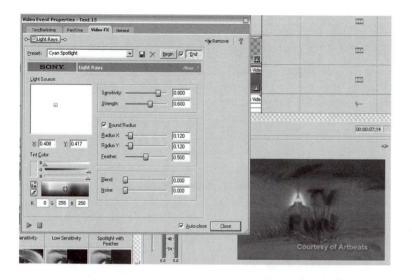

Courtesy of Artbeats

Add Pizzazz to Titles

Wish your titles would do something more? Drag and drop the Light Rays with the Intense preset from the Video FX tab of the window docking area to a title event.

Leave the preset parameters for the Begin point keyframe. Now select the End button. Click and drag the brown circle in the Light Position box from the lower right to the upper left. Preview how the Light Rays move across the title.

Use the Light Rays filter in a similar way. Add a title event and fade it in. Add the Cyan Spotlight preset to the title.

Start with the effect full on and then set to no effect for the End keyframe to recreate this effect. Or, split the event into multiple pieces for better control. Just be sure that the ending point of one event's FX are the same as the beginning of the next event's FX.

Cookie Cutter Cool

Place the same event on two adjacent video tracks. Drag and drop the 100 percent Black and White preset from the Black and White Video FX on the bottom event. Alternately, substitute Gaussian blur or Pixelate for the B/W FX.

Add the Cookie Cutter Video FX picture-in-picture preset to the top video event.

Adjust the position as needed. Color shows through where the box is while the rest of the video is black-and-white. Animate the box using the Begin/End to follow action.

Substitute Gaussian Blur for the Pixelate FX for a subtler result.

The "Cops" Effect

Rotate or adjust the aspect ratio on some stills as needed.

Need to hide an identity, license plate, product, body part, gesture, or other material? Place the same event on two adjacent video tracks, one on top of the other. Add the Large Pixelate preset to the top event.

Position the circle, resize, and feather as needed. Use Begin/End to follow the action. Also, animate the Pixelate filter to obscure more detail.

Add the cookie cutter Circle, Center preset to the top event. Change the Method to "Cut away section" by choosing from the drop-down list.

Extremely Quick Slideshow Production

Need to create a slideshow from a bunch of stills fast? Click Options> Preferences>Video and set "New still image length (seconds)" to the duration you want for each slide. Four or 5 is good.

Select all your images using Explorer or the Media pool and drag them to the video track. Add some music and you're finished!

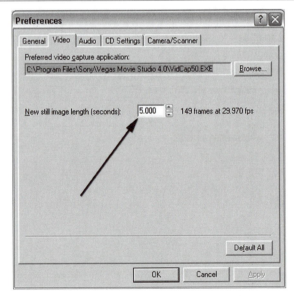

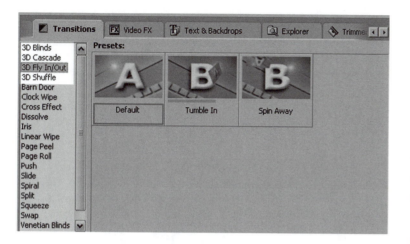

3D Transitions

Vegas Movie Studio includes several 3D transitions. Drag and drop them from the Transitions tab of the window docking area to an event fade-in, fade-out, or the crossfade between two events.

Use the Cross Effect and Zoom transitions on text that has been squeezed or pinched to create other 3D-like effects.

Reduce Red Eye in Still Photos

Vegas Movie Studio offers a feature to get rid of those pesky red eyes that plague some flash-photography shots.

If you have a photo that contains red eye, right-click the photo and choose Red Eye Reduction from the submenu.

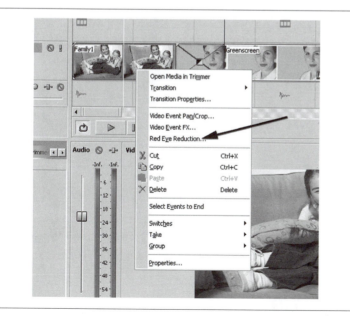

This dialog opens up. You'll need to zoom in on the red eye by using the + key on your keyboard or by using the + in the dialog box. Zoom in deeply on the eye.

Notice that inside this dialog, the cursor becomes a target indicator. Use this to draw a square around the red eye. You'll see a small aqua blue circle. This will define the area to be color-corrected for the red eye. This area may be resized by dragging the handles to size the target area. Be sure to contain only the red-eye area and not the rest of the subject's face.

Close the dialog box when you are finished. You can always reopen the dialog by right-clicking and choosing Red Eye Reduction again. When you've applied Red Eye Reduction to a still image, Vegas Movie Studio will remember your red-eye positioning even if you remove the image from the Timeline.

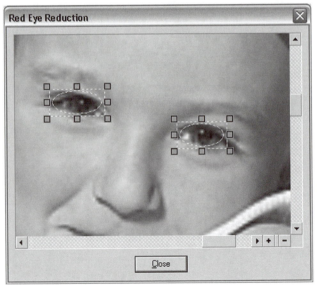

Chapter 9

Show Your Stuff

You've labored over your audio and video, and now it's time to deliver your latest masterpiece to the world. This chapter features tips for printing back to DV tape, rendering to a variety of formats including DVD, and preparing for web streaming.

Why Render?

As we pointed out earlier, Vegas Movie Studio uses project files, keeping the media separate. Therefore, to distribute the finished product, all the individual components—video, stills, titles, graphics, and sound—need to be rendered or compiled together as one finished video file. This is similar to baking a cake after you've compiled all the ingredients into the mixing bowl.

Rendering is a non-real-time process, sometimes faster but potentially significantly slower than the project's final length. Render times depend on the project and the hardware. The more complex the video, such as one with many transitions, FX, and mixed media types, the longer it takes to render. The faster the computer, the quicker the render time. For example, it may take a few seconds to render a five-minute, audio-only piece, and several hours to render a one-minute video.

Tip: Make the render the only computing task to decrease render times. Close all other programs, stop surfing the Net, etc.

The rendering process is the same whether your final output is destined for tape, DVD, or the web. Only the particular file formats change.

- DV—render to the same DV codec as the camcorder using the AVI format.

- DVD—render to MPEG-2, the standard format for DVDs.

- Print to tape (PTT)—render and copy the file to tape using the DV format (see above).

- QuickTime—render to the Apple-supported format.

- SVCD—render to MPEG-2 with lower resolution than DVD and deliver on CD-R.

- Uncompressed—render to full resolution, 4:4:4 video using the AVI format. These files are huge and will not play in real time. Useful as an archiving solution or when upsampling to HD.

- VCD—render to MPEG-1 and deliver on a CD-R. Many DVD players can play VCDs which hold up to 60 minutes of video that is near VHS quality.

- Web—render to web streaming formats such as Real Media, Windows Media, and QuickTime.

- YUV—render to a compressed, 4:2:2 lossless format smaller than uncompressed video and also suitable for archiving and upscaling and upsampling.

Click the Make Movie icon in the Toolbar or choose File>Make Movie to access the Make Movie—Select Destination dialog box. There are several choices:

- Save it to your hard drive—renders to a variety of formats to the hard drive location of your choice. We'll talk about customizing those in the next few pages.

- Burn it to DVD—launches Sonic MyDVD for authoring and encoding

- Burn it to Video CD (VCD) or CD-ROM—renders and copies the files to a standard CD-R

- Publish it to the web—renders to a variety of web-based streaming formats

- Save it to Sony devices—renders and places the file on the Sony device of your choice

- Save it to your camcorder's DV tape—renders and then prints to tape (just the opposite of capture)

- Email it—renders to smaller, lower-quality files for sending as email attachments

- Create an HTML page that includes it—renders to a web format and creates the page so others can access the video

Refer to the following sections for specific tips.

Print to Tape (PTT)

Connect your DV camcorder as though you were capturing footage. Make sure you insert either a blank DV tape or navigate to the point where you wish to record the file.

Click the Make Movie Button or choose File>Make Movie.

If any of the video is not already in the DV format, it will need to be pre-rendered before the PTT will begin. If that is only a few titles, transitions, and so forth, this is no big deal. The render will be fast and the PTT successful.

However, if your project is highly complex, render the file to the hard drive *before* using PTT (see below).

Files are always rendered completely before PTT. We recommend using the Make Movie>Save it to your hard drive option first and choosing the NTSC DV template.

When that operation completes, use the Make Movie>Save it to your camcorder's DV tape option. Check Use an Existing File and enter the file name and path.

To print to tape from an existing file, launch Video capture through File> Capture Video or click the Capture Video button in the Media Pool. Navigate to the Print to Tape tab.

PTT will overwrite any existing video on a tape. Use a blank tape or cue the camcorder to the proper place on an existing tape.

Click the Add Files button and choose the file or files to PTT.

The operation stops automatically when the files end or when manually ended.

From the PTT tab of the Capture dialog, choose File>Open and select the video file to PTT. Cue the camcorder, then click the Record to Device button. The warning dialog reminds you that your tape should be blank or properly cued. Click Yes to continue, and the PTT begins.

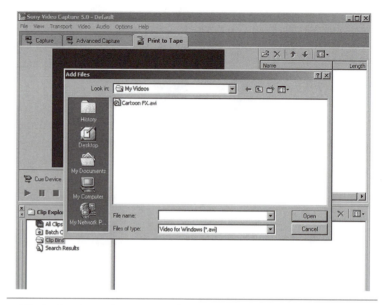

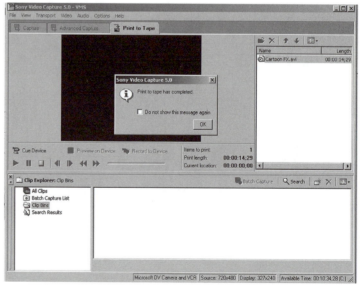

Render to a DV File on the Hard Drive

Click File>Make Movie to display the dialog box. Choose the Save it to Your Hard Drive option. From the "Save as type" drop-down list choose Video for Windows (*.avi). Choose a file path. Your render will usually be slightly faster if you render to a second system hard drive.

From the Template drop-down list, choose NTSC DV. This is the same DV format as your camcorder. If you are outside the United States or Japan, your system is likely PAL, and you'll need to select that format from the drop-down menu.

Substitute the PAL DV template if it applies.

Click Advanced Render, then the Custom Tab on the Render As dialog for more options. Typically, the default settings are ideal for the DV render.

Name the file, navigate to a location on your hard drive to store it, and then click Save to start the render process.

The dialog box indicates the render progress.

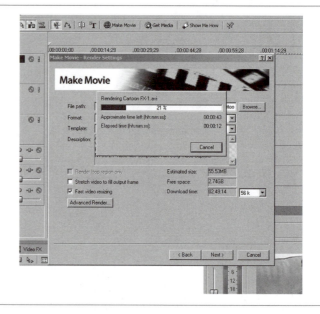

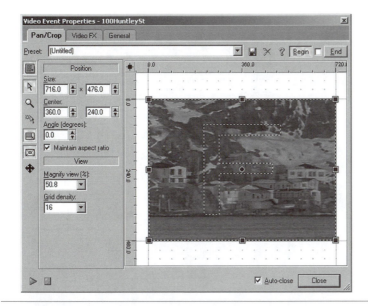

MPEG-2 Encoding Tips

The nature of MPEG-2 encoding means that getting a quality output requires a little more work on your part. There is often video noise along the outer screen edge. The encoder allocates resources to this junk. Eliminate the noise, and the encoder concentrates on your hard work instead. Also, reducing the color information results in a better encode.

Cropping and reducing saturation make web encodes look better, too.

Before rendering, prepare your video in two ways. One, crop the video slightly using Event Pan/Crop. Come in about six pixels from the edge—714×476 with "Maintain aspect ratio" turned on.

If the source was analog tape such as VHS, crop to eliminate the analog banding noise along the bottom.

Two, reduce the color saturation by 10 to 15 percent. Drop the HSL Adjust Video FX on the Preview window and set the saturation slider to between 0.85 and 0.90. This reduces the color slightly but ultimately makes the final MPEG-2 look better.

Render to DVD (MPEG-2)

DVDs must be authored separately, but you can render your file to the proper MPEG-2 format from Vegas. Click File> Make Movie to display the dialog box. From the dialog box choose Make Burn DVD.

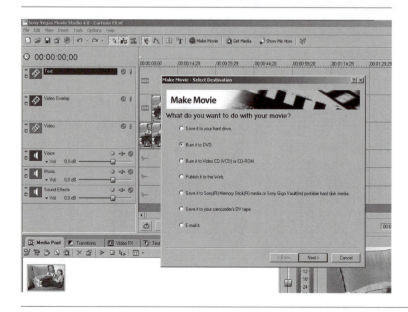

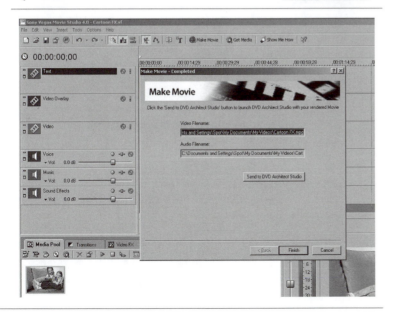

Click Next. From the Render Settings dialog, choose the names and locations of the rendered video and audio files.

Click the Custom button and navigate to the Video tab. Check the Two-pass option, and Vegas will go through the file twice, resulting in a higher-quality encode.

The render progress window will now appear.

Once the render completes, click the Send to DVD-Architect Studio button to author the final DVD.

Render for Web Streaming

From the File>Make Movie, choose Email It or Publish to the Web. Publish to Web will attempt to connect you to acidplanet.com to publish the file to the web. You will have only two choices for output if you use the Publish to the Web option. Choose RealMedia or Windows Media from the options presented.

Use the Email It template for most web renders. You'll have a number of options. Windows Media is the most common format, and the most playable format on the most number of computers.

Here you can choose from a variety of speeds (bitrates) and qualities. For most emailing, never use templates larger than 512kbps; and 256kbps is a fairly standard streaming bitrate, which usually won't be too large to mail.

Archiving Projects

Storing your work for the future is a necessary workflow. Obviously, just saving the project file isn't enough, as you need to save the media, too. And it may be in many different places.

Click File>Save As and then check "Copy all media with project."

Name the project and choose a storage location. Consider creating a new folder on a separate drive. Click OK. Now the project may be transported to another computer or burned to a DVD-data disk for archiving.

Burn a data CD or DVD of archived projects as another backup!

Archiving Format

DV uses 4:1:1 color space, MPEG-2 uses 4:2:0, and HDV uses 4:2:0. Therefore, the ideal archiving format is uncompressed video. Another alternative is the Sony YUV codec, which is 4:2:2 and creates smaller file sizes. It's great for re-rendering MPEG-2 files if necessary, and it upscales and upsamples well for moving content to the HD world.

Generally, you'll be just fine using DV compression for the final render format, one that you'll be able to edit later on. While Vegas Movie Studio is capable of rendering MPEG, and you can also edit MPEG in Vegas Movie Studio, MPEG is not a good format for editing. Archive to an AVI format; use the NTSC or PAL DV template for best results. If you ever plan on resampling or using the video for broadcast in other, higher-resolution formats, archive using the Uncompressed option found in Vegas Movie Studio. Your file will take a very long time to render, and it will use a lot of storage space, but the quality will be superb.

Chapter 10

Burn a DVD

In Vegas Movie Studio, you also should have installed the DVD Architect Studio software. This software will allow you to create professional DVD stylings. While not as robust as the much more expensive applications, DVD Architect Studio provides all the tools you need to create either template-driven DVDs or completely customized DVDs, with navigation just like the DVDs you buy at the video store. You can also create slideshows and video or audio compilations.

The main interface is where you'll be doing most of the work. Look for the Media Explorer as the location of all your video assets.

Before you create your DVD, consider mapping it out on paper. This helps create a more logical menu flow.

On the right side, you'll notice the Properties window. This is where you'll modify behaviors of the buttons, menus, compilations, and slideshows.

Start by dragging a media file that is an AVI, MOV, MPG, or WMV file from the Media Explorer to the Menu/main workspace and dropping it. This will create a button with the filename beneath it. The image will be the first frame of the video file.

If you prefer the button to be video-only, or if you'd rather it be text-only, right-click the button and choose Link/ Image Only or Link/Text Only. This will convert the button. Alternatively, in the Properties window, Object tab, you can select Text Only or Image Only from the drop-down menu.

If your video is like a lot of videos, the first frame is black. You might like the image to be something other than black. Go to the Properties window, Object tab on the right side of the screen. In this window, select the Thumbnail Start time slider. Move it to the right and you'll notice that the image in the button shifts. (If it doesn't move, you'll need to select the button you've dropped on the Menu).

Use graphics related to your DVD project as button images.

If you want the button to be a moving picture button or animated button, check the Animate Thumbnail checkbox. This will cause the button to play the contents of the video file.

By default, the Enable Frame checkbox is selected. This allows you to use any number of frames that are installed with DVD Architect Studio.

Some frames, like this circular frame you see here, may be animated. Select the Animated Frames from the Frames drop-down menu, and you'll be able to check the Animated Frames checkbox. These can spice up your menus if you want fancy menu button frames. Notice that you can choose the start point for animated frames just like you can choose the start point for animated buttons.

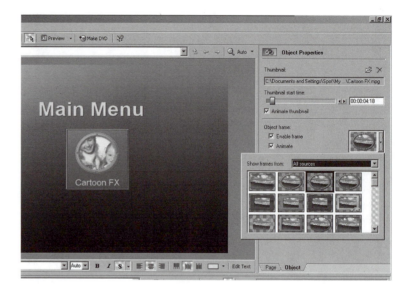

Next, in the Properties window, Page tab is a Modify Link button. Here you can modify what the button is linked to. So, you can define a thumbnail for the button but have it link to a video file not associated with that graphic.

Click the Modify Link button and notice that the Link Properties dialog opens. It will show the currently linked video and audio files. You can change the video file while leaving the audio file unchanged, or vice versa. Click the folder icon to browse for a different video or audio file, or click the red X to remove the audio or video file.

To return to the main menu, click the Back button or use the Backspace key on your keyboard.

Now repeat the process by dragging up your next button. As with the first button, you may use any frame, link, or thumbnail. Repeat this process until you've got all the buttons you'd like on the menu.

If you have more than six graphic buttons on a menu, consider creating a second menu to keep your menu from appearing to be cluttered.

Making Menus

In DVD Architect Studio, you can work with menus from one of two work-flows. First, you can use templates; this is the fastest and easiest method of working. Second, you can custom-design menus to look exactly as you'd like them.

First, we'll start by creating custom menus, as you've already started moving in that direction by using custom frames for the buttons. The two biggest differences between a custom menu and a template menu are the background and button styles.

DVD Architect Studio offers motion menus. This means you can create a video file in Vegas Movie Studio that can be used as a motion background.

Avoid superbright, super contrasted colors in your DVD menus. These colors will bleed on the typical television and are hard on the viewers' eyes.

It's recommended that video files for motion menus only be 30 to 60 seconds in length. To insert a motion background to your menu, locate the file you've created in Vegas Movie Studio, right-click and drag it to the menu/workspace. Choose Set Background Video and Audio from the drop-down menu.

You can also set a video-only file as the background and then select a different audio file for the audio background of your DVD.

To change the background audio, select the Properties window, Page tab, and click the File/Open button. Choose the audio file you'd like to use as the background audio for your menu.

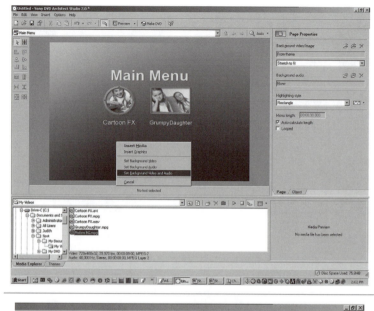

In this same dialog, you can set the length of the menu as well. Generally, this is automatically set to the length of the music, but you can specify the length by unchecking the Auto-Calculate Length checkbox and setting the length manually in the dialog box.

You can also make the menu loop so that it plays over and over. Check the Loop Menu checkbox to make a menu loop.

Looping menus prevent the screen from simply going dark or static, and they invite viewers to click a button.

Modifying Text

By default, all menus are named "Menu" in DVD Architect. Obviously, you won't want all your menus to be labeled as "Menu." To modify any text in a menu, either select the text and press the F2 key, or right-click and chose Edit Text. Note that there is an Edit Text button at the lower right of the workspace.

Make changes to text, fonts, size, add a shadow, change the color, do whatever you'd like to do with the text.

You can resize the text with the Resize tool as well.

Perhaps your text, buttons, or other asset links aren't lined up properly. Holding the Ctrl key, select all the assets you'd like to align. On the left side of the workspace, you'll find a number of alignment tools. You can align to the bottom, top, left or right side, center the text and buttons, or make all text and buttons the same size.

This is very handy if you've got a lot of menu options or text links that you need to line up to one side or the other. These tools will help you make your menu neat and clean.

Hidden Highlights!

Have you noticed how buttons in the movies you rent or buy from the video store have highlights around or beneath them? You can accomplish this same level of coolness in DVD Architect Studio. To create highlights, select the image or text button that you'd like to highlight. In the Properties window, Page tab you'll notice a Highlighting Style drop-down menu option. Here, you can select several highlighting styles.

Use animated buttons to illustrate what the scene or video contains. Consider creating short videos just for buttons, featuring highlights of the scene.

- Rectangle—Highlights all buttons with a rectangular overlay

- Mask Overlay—Highlights the button with a highlight in the shape of the button

- Underline—Underlines either the button or text associated with button

- Text Rectangle—Highlights the text with a rectangle

- Text Mask Overlay—Uses the shape of the font to create a mask

- Image Rectangle—Creates a rectangle over only the image portion of the button

- —Image Mask Overlay—Creates a mask using the shape of the image button

In this illustration you can see the Underline Highlight selected.

Keep in mind that all buttons or links on the menu will be assigned this overlay and highlight style. DVD Architect 3.0 that comes with Sony Vegas offers the ability to use different button highlights for each button.

The button highlight by default, is a half-opacity white color. You can modify the color of the highlight to suit your desire. To the right of the Highlighting drop-down menu you'll find a color palette menu button.

Select the desired color from this drop-down menu. It's best if you keep the opacity less than 75 percent if you want to allow the button to show through when the image is highlighted. In this image, the highlight is improperly set to 100 percent opaque.

In this image, the opacity is properly set to 60 percent, but you can use any opacity provided it's less than 90 percent. Of course, if your intent is to block the text or button, then by all means, use 100 percent opacity.

Satisfying Slideshows

DVD Architect Studio can assist you in building wonderful and fun slideshows. These are very fast and easy to create.

Right-click the workspace/menu, and from the drop-down menu, select Insert Picture Slideshow. You can also use the Ctrl+L shortcut to accomplish the same thing.

This places a new button on the workspace. The Slideshow button can be either a text-only or image-only button.

Double-click the button to open the Compilation dialog. You'll see an area to the right for the Slideshow Properties.

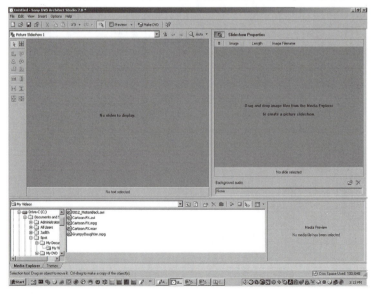

This is where you'll drag your images for the slideshow. You can drag several images at one time.

You can also reorder the images by simply dragging the files around, placing them in the order you'd like them to appear.

Look closely at the order of the images and see the changes.

Often, slides, stills, and graphics don't properly fit the aspect ratio of the television screen. DVD Architect Studio has tools to help you fix this.

If you have an image that doesn't meet the aspect ratio, you have three options available:

1. Letterbox—leaves the image at its natural aspect, putting black letterboxing or pillarboxing to fit screen.

2. Stretch to fit—stretches images across the screen. This doesn't work well with tall pictures, as they'll make the subjects appear short and fat as seen in this illustration.

3. Zoom to fit—often the best option, this zooms in on the middle of the subject, causing it to fit the screen. It can cut the heads and feet off subjects.

You can cause all images to match aspect ratio by clicking the top image, holding the Shift key, and clicking on the last image in your slideshow. This will match the aspect equally on all images.

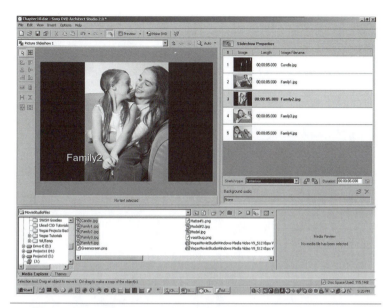

If the picture is rotated to one side or the other, you can rotate the image to fit the screen the way you'd like to. Click the Rotate Counter-Clockwise or Clockwise button found next to the Stretch to Fit option. This will rotate the image the direction so it displays correctly.

You can time the slideshow to music if you'd like. Find an audio file that you'd like to have as an accompaniment to the slideshow, by using the Background Audio Browse button.

Next to the image length field (Duration), you'll find the Fit Slideshow to Audio button. Clicking this button will auto-time the slideshow to the length of the audio. If you don't want to match the length to an audio file, you can determine the length of all slides or individual slides. Click on a slide or group of slides, and input the time in the Length Field.

Music Compilations

DVD Architect also allows you to create music compilations. This means you can grab a collection of your favorite songs and create a DVD of those songs for playing in your DVD player or laptop computer.

Right-click the menu/workspace and choose Insert Music Compilation. You can also use the keyboard shortcut, Ctrl+K.

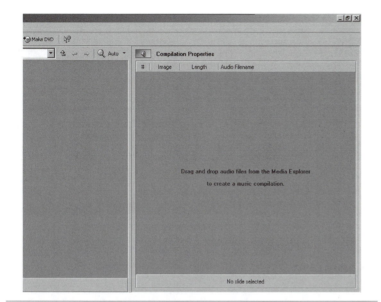

This will insert a new button on the menu/workspace. Double-click this button to open the Music Compilation properties page.

You can drag as many musical files as you'd like to the Compilation Properties dialog. These files will be rendered as PCM files, so you'll want to keep size in mind.

You can also use a graphic to show during playback of the audio file. Each audio file may have its own graphic. This is a good place to display album art or an image related to the song that's playing.

Drag an image file from the Explorer to the song in the Music Compilation Properties box. This image will display during the playback of the music file.

You can also have Video Compilations, although DVD Architect Studio doesn't mention it by name. Drag video files to the Music Compilations Properties dialog just as you drag audio files. The video files will play in sequence. You can rearrange the video playlist just as you can rearrange the audio playlist, by dragging files in order of priority in the Compilation Properties dialog.

Preview the DVD

Before you burn the DVD or continue on the authoring path, you might want to preview the DVD so you have an idea of how it's going to look when you burn it to a final DVD. DVD Architect Studio gives you all the tools you need to preview the project.

Save your project (it's a good idea to save your project periodically) and then preview it by pressing the F9 key, or clicking the Preview button. You can either preview just the menu page, or by pressing Ctrl+F9, preview the entire project. The Preview window opens up.

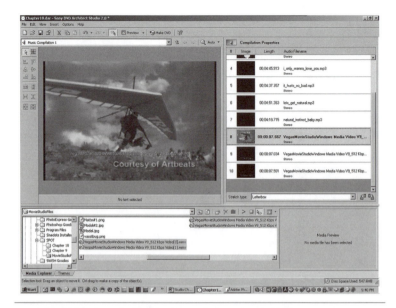

The remote control to the right side of the window is used just like a remote control on a set-top DVD player. Although you can navigate the menu using your mouse, it's highly recommended that you navigate with the remote so you can check the behavior of the DVD project as it will be viewed on a regular TV and set-top player.

Don't forget to check for button alignment and thumbnails. Check each and every link to be sure that your DVD flows like it should.

Advanced Menus

In Hollywood-authored DVDs, you'll notice that there are often submenus. DVD Architect Studio offers many of the same features. These submenus can act as scene selection menus, additional sales information, contact information, or other valuable add-ons to your video.

Before creating a submenu, let's create chapter points in a video file to which your submenu can point. Double-click any video file you've dragged to the menu/workspace that currently has a button. This opens the file in the Timeline view.

In the Timeline window that opens, you can create chapter markers or scene pointers. Put the cursor where you'd like a scene marker to occur, and press the M key to insert a marker.

This will tell the DVD authoring application where to go when a button pointing to a scene is selected. It also allows viewers to press their "Skip" button. You can also give the chapters a name, and this name will show up in the submenu when you create it, and DVD Architect Studio will auto-link these names to the chapters. Right-click the button linking to the video for which you've just inserted the chapter markers on the main menu page, and choose Insert Scene Selection Menu.

A dialog opens, asking you how many scenes you'd like the new page to have and for a name of the new page. If you don't name the menu page here, you can name it later.

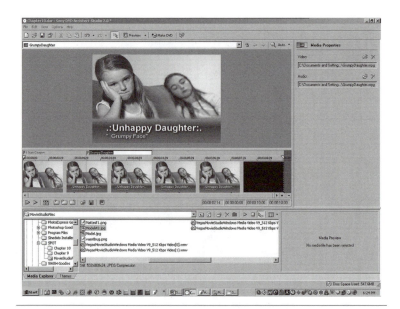

This will create a new button on the Timeline. Double-click this button, and a new menu page will open.

Notice that the scenes are already named and numbered for you, based on the chapter markers that you created earlier. There is by default, a red arrow already in the scene selection menu. This arrow is linked to the main menu. You can change the arrow by clicking the Object Properties tab and choosing a different arrow. You can also specify a custom arrow. PNG format with transparency is best, but any image may be used.

You can also insert a link to custom menus with no chapter points. This might be used to create links to other videos that are different than the main selection. To insert a submenu, right-click the menu/workspace and choose Insert Submenu or use the Ctrl+M shortcut. This will open a new menu.

You can drag any asset to this menu that you'd like, including creating still more submenus, picture compilations, music compilations, video playlists, or links to text pages. For instance, you could create a link button to a text-only page that had contact information for you as the author of the DVD, or a sales page for the product that you might be displaying in the DVD.

Burn Baby Burn!

Now that you've assembled the components of the DVD and previewed it several times to ensure that all links are working, you're ready to burn your DVD with the application.

Click the Make DVD button found at the top of the workspace. A dialog opens up, prompting you to Prepare DVD, Burn DVD, or Prepare and Burn DVD.

Use Prepare DVD if you don't wish to burn the project at this time. You will be required to re-prepare the DVD if you decide to make any changes at this point.

The Burn DVD option may be used only if you've previously prepared the DVD to a folder and can locate that prepared folder.

Use the Prepare and Burn DVD if you're ready to burn the DVD at this point. Click your choice, and then click Next. This dialog opens up.

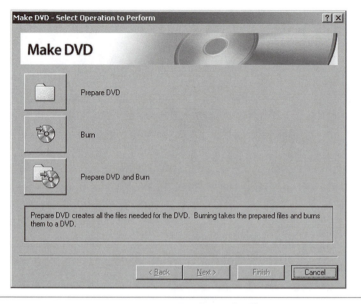

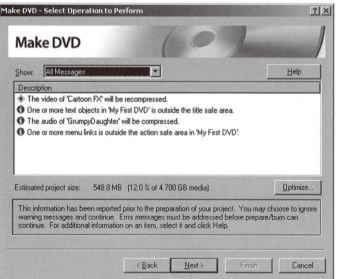

Make DVD - Select Folder

Make DVD

Prepare folder: C:\Documents and Settings\Spot\My DVD\   Browse...

Free storage space in selected folder: 2,689.3 Megabytes

Select the folder where you want the DVD to be prepared to.

< Back   Next >   Finish   Cancel

This dialog will tell you that certain components (or all components) of your DVD need to be compressed. This is normal. DVD Architect Studio is simply telling you that you have assets in the project that don't comply with DVD specifications. Video must be MPEG-2 to be burned to a compliant DVD. If you have AVI, MOV, WMV, or other file formats, DVD Architect must convert these files to the MPEG-2 format. If you have menus with non-MPEG-2 components, then the menus will be converted to the MPEG-2 format as well. This screen is telling you it will convert listed files. Click the Next button.

This dialog will offer the option to choose a Prepare folder. Choose a location that you'll be able to find later, preferably on a drive different than your system drive. This is where the DVD will be rendered to and stored. When you click the Finish button, the DVD will begin to render. If you have chosen the Prepare and Burn DVD option, the DVD will render and then burn. If you have chosen the Prepare DVD, you'll be able to point to this file later and burn at your own leisure.

You may have noticed an Optimize button when you chose the Prepare DVD or Prepare and Burn DVD. This button is there to set a bitrate for your project. By default, DVD Architect Studio will determine the best bitrate for your project. However, DVD Architect Studio will also allow you to override the default bitrate for select features. For example, you might have a long movie that you want at a high bitrate, and also have some lesser videos such as "coming up" or "additional titles" types of media. You might need those at a lower bitrate so that the longer video will fit. Therefore, you might want those at a bitrate of 3000kbps for instance.

Click this file and check the Override checkbox.

Note that the default bitrate is 8000kbps. Never go above this bitrate, you might find systems that simply can't play these high-speed files back properly. When you've finished instructing DVD Architect Studio as to how you'd like to override settings, click the OK button and proceed as described above.

Never have bitrates faster than 8000kbps. Some computer systems will have difficulty playing files that have higher bitrates.

Chapter 11

ACID: Making Music

ACID Music Studio is a highly graphical program that can be used on many levels. Nonlinear editors can use it for scoring video, drawing on the enormous talent of the loop creators and assemble a musical composition simply by painting loops on the Timeline. Musicians can augment existing loops by recording their own loops or by using ACID as you would any recording software to create entire tracks that don't loop.

Loops, One-Shots, and Beatmaps

ACID maintains properties in the metadata of a wave file that tells it how to interpret that wave when it is brought into ACID. The process of adding this metadata as known as ACIDization or to ACIDize. ACIDized files can be Loops, one-shots, or beatmaps.

If you are creating music for video, you should set the audio properties of your project to 48,000Hz sample rate and 16-bit depth. This is the same rate that DV video uses for audio.

• **Loops:** wave files that are usually only one or two measures in length, although the metadata allows for up to 41 measures. The properties maintained for loops are the root note for transposing, and the number of beats for time stretching. There is a special value for the root note called "Don't transpose." This used for loops that should not respond to key changes like drum loops.

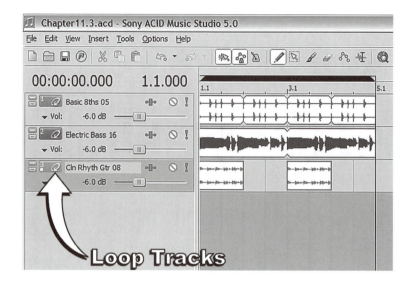

- **One-Shot:** a wave file that does not loop and has no concept of tempo. These are used for hits like cymbal crashes, or single drum or instrument sounds. They play for their duration and then stop. One-shots of instruments like bass guitars can be useful in creating melodic bass patterns using pitch shift.

- **Beatmapped tracks:** longer files more than 30 seconds in length. These are usually entire songs that have their tempo mapped to a beat. The properties maintained for beatmapped tracks are the root note for transposing, the tempo in beats per minute (BPM), and the offset of the first downbeat. Beatmapped tracks also have a "Don't transpose" value for their root note. This is used when beatmapping songs that you may want to make slower or faster in tempo but don't want the key to change.

ACID can also read and write MIDI files.

- **MIDI tracks:** tracks that contain MIDI files instead of audio files. They behave like loop tracks in that the events repeat when sized beyond their end. They also respond to tempo data. If you set their root key to something other than "Don't transpose" they with respond to key change data, too.

All of the compositions that you create in ACID Music Studio will be built from a combination of these four building blocks. Each of these loop types resides in a track of the same type. You can only have one media file on each track, so it may take several tracks of drums, bass, guitar, etc., to make up the parts you want for your song.

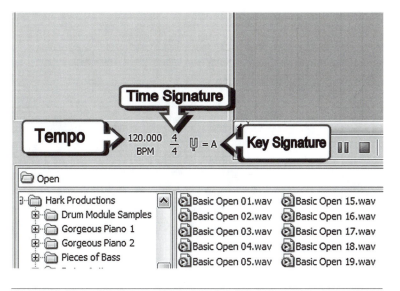

Tempo and Key

You can set up the initial tempo, key, and time signature by selecting the respective interface controls as shown the picture. It's a good idea to do this for each project, otherwise ACID will default all your projects to 120bpm, 4/4 time in the key of A. ACID will automatically pitch shift any loops you add to the project to match the key you have selected. Tempo and key changes can be made within the project.

To quickly add loops to an ACID project, just double-click on them from the Explorer window.

Preview, Pick, Paint, and Play

You can compose music by simply dragging loops from the ACID Explorer window into the track window and then painting them on the new track.

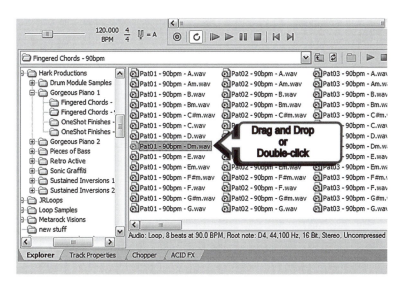

Start by selecting the Explorer tab at the bottom left of the ACID Music Studio interface. From the Explorer you can navigate to the files and folders on your hard drive. When you click on a music file it will play so that you can preview it. The bottom of the file display will show you the following information about the wave file:

- The type of ACID wave file

- How many beats it contains

- How many beats per minute

- Root note (if any)

- Sample frequency

- Sample bit depth

This information is useful because although ACID Music Studio can time-stretch your loops to match the tempo of your song, too much time-stretching will result in unwanted artifacts during playback.

1. Drag a file and drop it on the Timeline area or double-click it to add it to the Timeline.

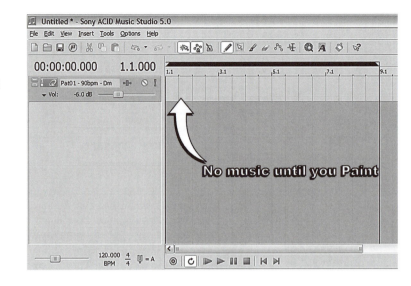

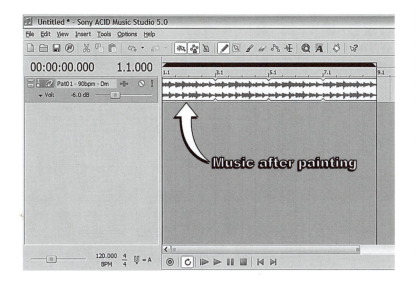

A new empty track will appear for this loop. If you press the Play from Start (Shift+F12) button, nothing will play. Why? Because ACID has loaded the loop into an empty track, but it doesn't know where you want to play the loop. You must paint or draw the events on the track to tell ACID when to play the loop.

You can replace the loop in a track by dragging a new loop to the track header and dropping it.

2. Select the Draw tool (Ctrl+D) if it isn't already selected—it's the one that looks like a pencil.

3. Drag the Draw tool across the track you just created to paint events on it.

ACID will draw the loop for as long as you continue dragging. This is how you tell ACID where to play the loop on the Timeline. Now if you place the Timeline cursor at the beginning of the loop event and press the Play button you will hear the loop play in the tempo and key of the project.

You can draw events anywhere on the Timeline with spaces between them. This allows you to control exactly when a loop will play and when it will not. To play the project from the current cursor position, use the spacebar. Press the spacebar again to stop it.

One of the biggest errors beginning users make is that they forget the paint part. ACID won't make any sounds unless you paint the loops on the tracks.

4. Drop a second loop onto the Timeline.

Try to select one that is a different number of beats, or BPM, or key (root note). Use the data display at the bottom of the Explorer window to determine this.

5. Use the Draw tool again to paint events onto the Timeline.

6. Click Play or press the spacebar.

You should hear the two loops play in sync and in the same key even though their BPM and root notes may have been different. ACID will adjust loops to play together so that you don't have to worry about these things. This is why the properties in the ACIDized loops are so important.

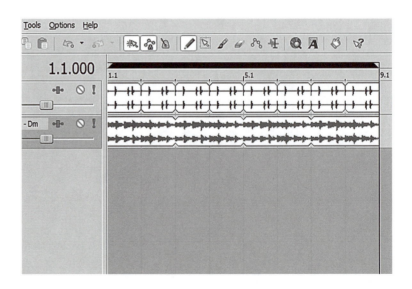

Notice there is a little divot that displays at regular intervals in the event; these are the places where the wave file is looping. If you selected two loops that contained a different number of beats as we did in the example, the divots will display at different intervals. The top track has a loop length of four beats while the bottom track has a loop length of eight beats.

You can also paint loops on the Timeline with the Paint tool—it looks like a paintbrush. You don't have to drag the Paint tool to place events on the Timeline. Just a *left-click* of the mouse will paint for one grid duration. Unlike the Draw tool, the Paint tool works on multiple tracks without lifting the mouse. You can quickly paint a vertical set of events across tracks using the Paint tool.

To quickly paint a loop, beatmapped, or one-shot file on the Timeline for its full duration use Shift+Paint tool.

You don't have to be too concerned about painting an event beyond the point you want it to end. You can always adjust the event size after it's been drawn or painted by using the Draw tool and hovering it over either end of the event. The arrow cursor will turn into the resize cursor, and clicking and holding the left mouse button will allow you to adjust the length of the event.

The Erase tool will also remove parts of an event equal to the current grid increment.

Loop Sources

ACID is only as good as the loops you buy for it. The greatest source of loops is the Sony Sound Series available at: http://mediasoftware.sonypictures. com/loop_libraries

There are also many third-party loop libraries that offer high-quality loops.

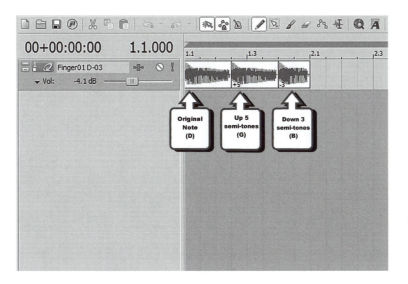

Some of our favorites are:

- Hark Productions,
  www.harkproductions.com/loops

- Smart Loops,
  www.smartloops.com

- Big Fish Audio,
  www.bigfishaudio.com

Many of these sites offer free sample loops so you can download a few and judge the quality of the loops for yourself.

Creating Solos, Melodies, and Themes

You can create interesting solos and melodies from existing loops using slicing and pitch shifting. Existing loops can be split and sliced into sections, while one-shots can simply be pitch shifted in place.

To change the melody of a loop:

1. Paint one cycle of the loop on the Timeline.

Use Shift+(+/−) to shift four semitones and Ctrl+(+/−) to shift an octave (12 semitones).

2. Use the S key to split out the part whose pitch you want to change.

3. Highlight the split section and use the + or − keys to pitch shift to a new note.

You can slice the loop in several pieces and copy and paste slices to repeat sections you like. This is like creating an entirely new loop. One-shots can be used to create a solo or melody by individually pitch shifting them.

Once you have a melody that you like, you can use Paste Repeat to copy it across the track. To do this:

1. Select the loop events you want to repeat. (Hint: use Shift+Select to select a group.)

2. Press Ctrl+C to copy these events to the clipboard.

3. Position your cursor at the place on the Timeline you want to start repeating the events.

4. Select Edit>Paste Repeat (Ctrl+B) to bring up the Paste Repeat dialog.

5. Choose the number of times to paste and paste spacing. Select even spacing, and paste every one measure (for a loop that is one measure in length).

6. Press OK, and the events will be pasted at each measure for the number of times indicated.

> **You could also solo the track, loop the events, and use Ctrl+M to render to a new track using the "Render loop region only" option.**

Recording in ACID

You can record both audio and MIDI in ACID Music Studio. The procedure is the same for both.

To record audio:

1. Click the Record button on the transport or press Ctrl+R.

2. Make sure the Record Type is set to Audio.

3. In the Record dialog, select the name of the file and directory you want the recording to be placed in.

4. Optionally, change the start position and turn on the metronome.

5. Check to make sure the correct

recording device is selected. Use the meters on the left to be sure you have a good signal.

6. Click the Record button to start recording. It will change to a Stop button to stop recording. Click Stop when you are done.

If you are recording music to be included in a video, your record attributes should be set to 48,000Hz, 16-bit. This is the same rate that DV video uses on its audio track.

If you want to record MIDI using the internal DLS Soft Synth, you must first insert one.

To insert the DLS Soft Synth:

• Choose Insert>Soft Synth or click the Insert Soft Synth button above the master fader.

A new DLS Soft Synth will be inserted into the Buss area. You can insert several DLS Soft Synths and load new DLS sounds into them. DLS sounds can be purchased or found on the Internet. Each DLS Soft Synth is multitimbral and can process 16 MIDI channels of data at once.

To record MIDI:

1. Click the Record button on the transport or press Ctrl+R.

2. Make sure the Record Type is set to MIDI.

3. In the Record dialog, select the name of the file and directory you want the recording to be placed in.

4. Optionally, change the start position and turn on the metronome.

5. Check to make sure the correct recording device is selected. This should be set to the MIDI device that your controller is connected to. The MIDI Thru setting allows you to select the proper Soft Synth or MIDI output.

6. Click the Record button to start recording. It will change to a Stop button to stop recording. Click the Stop button when done.

The default record location will be determined by your settings in Options> Preferences> Folders.

Scoring to Video

ACID has the ability to work with video so that you can easily score music to it. There is one video track that can hold a single video file. This should be either a rough cut or final cut rendered from your NLE. The video track is always pinned to the top of the Timeline so that it is always visible.

To add a video to ACID:

• Choose File>Open and select the video file from the file system or just drag and drop a video file from Windows Explorer into the ACID Timeline.

The audio will be added as a one-shot so that ACID will not time-stretch it in any way.

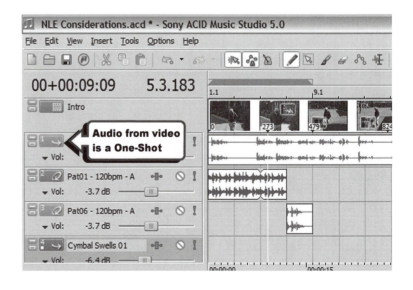

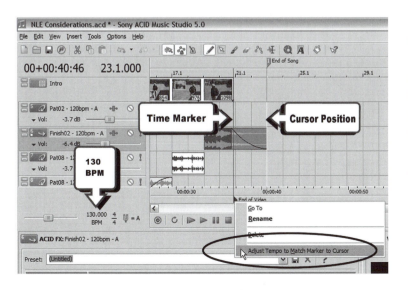

For scoring for video, it is important to know the difference between time markers and beat markers. Time markers are tied to absolute wall-clock time. Unlike beat markers, they stay locked to the video and always represent the true time that has transpired since the beginning of the project. This is critical for scoring video because your video is running at a constant real-time rate. Beat markers stick to the measure and beat of the music regardless of tempo or time.

To Insert a time marker:

• Select the menu item Insert>Time Marker or press H.

Notice that the time marker is placed at the bottom of the Timeline where the time ruler is. Time markers can have labels just like any other marker by right-clicking them and selecting Rename. When marking events in the video that you want to score to always use time markers.

ACID has an incredible time saver for getting a musical event to match the exact moment of a video event. It's called Adjust Tempo to Match Marker to Cursor. This allows you to place a time marker where you want a musical event to happen in the video, then place the cursor on the actual musical event, and it will adjust the tempo so that the event happens right on the time marker.

To map multiple events to time markers, place tempo markers on the musical events so that each will have its own tempo associated with it.

To use this feature, press H to place a time marker at the place in the video where you want the event to occur. For this example, we will select the end of the video clip.

Place the cursor on the audio event that must happen at the marker. For this example, we will place the cursor at the end of the music.

Right-click on the marker tab and select Adjust Tempo to Match Marker to Cursor.

ACID will adjust the preceding tempo marker (or the project tempo if there are no tempo markers) so that the events happen in sync.

Chapter 12

ACID to the Nth Degree

ACID Music Studio gives you the tools to add the finishing touches to your music by adding effects, arranging, and changing keys and tempos to make your music more exciting. When you're musically satisfied with your composition, you can mix it and render it as a music file to include in your video or burn it to CD.

Using FX

You can add FX to any loop or one-shot audio track. Audio FX cannot be applied to beatmapped or MIDI tracks. ACID FX include Distortion, EQ, a Low-Frequency Oscillator (LFO) to produce Chorus, Flanger, Phaser, or Wah-Wah, a Delay, and a Reverb.

To apply FX to a track:

1. Click the Track FX button in the track header (or select the ACID FX tab in the lower left of the ACID interface with the track selected).

2. Check the checkbox for the FX you want to apply to the track and adjust the FX settings in the ACID FX window.

Tempo-based effects enable you to make effects that cycle (such as echoes and chorus) on musical tempo boundaries without having to calculate the actual timing manually—which changes as the tempo changes. ACID Music Studio has two tempo FX: LFO (Chorus, Flange, Phaser, Wah-Wah) and Delay.

To use a tempo FX, set the LFO Clock or Delay to Tempo instead of Time. Then select the musical boundary you want (such as measure or quarter note). A big advantage of using tempo over time is that the tempo will remain relative as the tempo of the song changes so that the LFO or Delay remain musically in sync.

You can save FX as presets so that you can recall them later or use them on a number of tracks. To save a preset:

1. Type a name for the preset in the Preset: entry field.

2. Click the Save Preset icon (diskette).

You can apply any FX preset to a track by selecting the track and recalling the FX preset from the Preset drop-down list on the ACID FX tab.

Arranging Parts

You can cut and paste parts to rearrange them on the Timeline using the Time Selection tool. The toolbar icon for the Time Selection tool is a blue wave with an I-beam on top of it.

To cut or copy a part of the Timeline:

1. Select the Time Selection tool.

2. Make a Timeline selection over the part you want to cut or copy.

3. Use the menu item Edit>Cut (Ctrl+X) or Edit>Copy (Ctrl+C) to cut or copy the part to the clipboard.

To paste the part at a new place on the Timeline:

- Use Paste (Ctrl+V) to apply it to an empty section. It will replace what is there.

- Use Paste Insert (Ctrl+Shift+V) to make room for the new part pushing everything to the right on the Timeline.

Changing Tempo and Key

You can also change the tempo, key, and time signature during the song by adding a Tempo/Key/Time Signature Change marker.

To change the tempo, key, or time signature of a song:

1. Place the cursor at the point on the Timeline where you want the change to take place.

2. Press T to change the tempo, K to change the key, or Shift+K to change the time signature.

3. Type the new values into the Tempo/Key/Time Signature Change dialog. You can change them all at the same time by enabling all three features.

4. Click OK to make the change.

When you play your song, the change you selected will happen when the playback cursor reaches that marker. A tempo change will either speed up or slow down a song; a key change will time-stretch all events that have a root key defined; and a time signature change will adjust the time ruler divisions and grid spacing on the Timeline as well as the downbeat of the metronome.

If you want a song to change tempo gradually, place several tempo markers at regular intervals with each one having a BPM value closer to the desired tempo.

Mixing (Level, EQ, Pan, FX)

All mixing in ACID Music Studio is done at the track level.

When you approach a mix, start with the percussion and mute the other tracks that you're not mixing. This will allow you to just concentrate on one instrument group at a time. Get all the instruments in a group level with each other first. Use Shift+Select to select more than one track at a time. This will allow you to adjust multiple track volumes in unison. Once all of one instrument are mixed, unmute the next group and bring it into the mix. Add any EQ or other FX as needed to sweeten the mix.

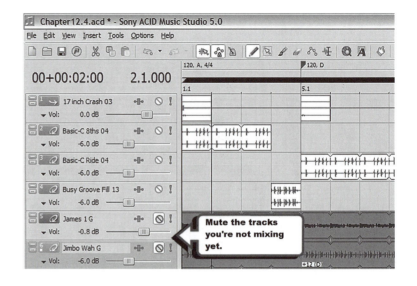

Mute the tracks you're not mixing yet.

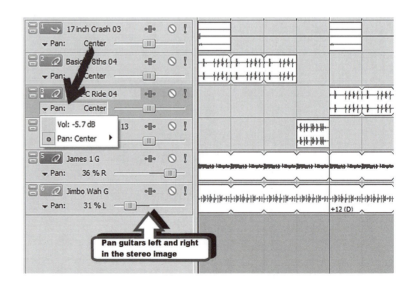

Pan guitars left and right in the stereo image

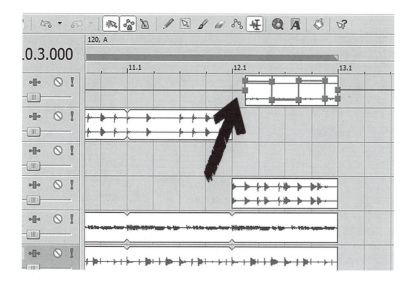

Switch the volume sliders to Pan and spread out the stereo image by placing instruments like guitars and keyboards slightly left and right of center. To do this:

1. Click on the VOL label in the track header.

2. Select Pan from the drop-down list.

3. Adjust the Pan sliders to spread instruments out in the stereo image.

You can insert a volume or pan envelope on any track to control volume and pan over time. To do this for pan (volume is the same):

1. Right-click on the track and select Insert/Remove Envelope>Pan (a pan envelope will be displayed)

2. Double-click on the envelope to add an adjustment point where you want the pan to start.

3. Double-click on the envelope to add an adjustment point where you want the pan to end.

4. Adjust the points for the amount of pan desired.

You can insert a volume envelope on the master bus if you need your song to fade out. To add a volume envelope to the master bus:

1. Press the B key to show the master bus.

2. Right-click in the Timeline area of the master bus and Select Insert/Remove Envelope>Volume (Shift+V). A volume envelope will be inserted and displayed.

3. Double-click on the volume envelope to add a point where you want it to start fading out.

4. Double-click on the volume envelope to add a point where the song should be completely faded.

5. Adjust the last volume envelope point to –Inf.

Export Finished Songs

You can render your final project as a WAV file, MP3, or other media format, or you can burn it directly to CD. If you are going to use it in Vegas Movie Studio, the best format to use is a WAV file at 48kHz, 16-bit. This is the same sample rate that DV video uses.

To export your song:

1. Select File>Render As.

2. In the Render As dialog, enter a name for your song.

3. Select a Save Type. If saving for video select Wave (Microsoft) (*.wav).

4. Select a Template for that type. For DV video, use 48,000Hz, 16-Bit, Stereo, PCM.

5. Click Save.

ACID Music Studio gives you two options for burning your project on CD. You can fill up a CD one track at a time; this is known as track-at-once (TAO) burning. You may also burn your project as a single CD image with multiple tracks. This is known as disc-at-once (DAO) burning. The process is similar for both.

To burn a CD using the track-at-once method:

1. Load recordable CD media into your CD-RW drive.

2. Select Tools>Burn Track-at-once Audio CD.

3. In the Action drop-down select "Burn audio."

4. In the Drive drop-down select your CD-RW drive.

5. Click Start.

To burn disc-at-once, insert track markers using the N key where you want the tracks to begin. Then follow the steps above, selecting Tools>Burn Disc-at-once Audio CD in Step 2.

diate, accessible and thorough information. We offer a variety of training materials for different learning styles.

Whether you are looking for a book, a DVD, or an on-site trainer, VASST can provide tips, techniques, and solutions for all your media needs.

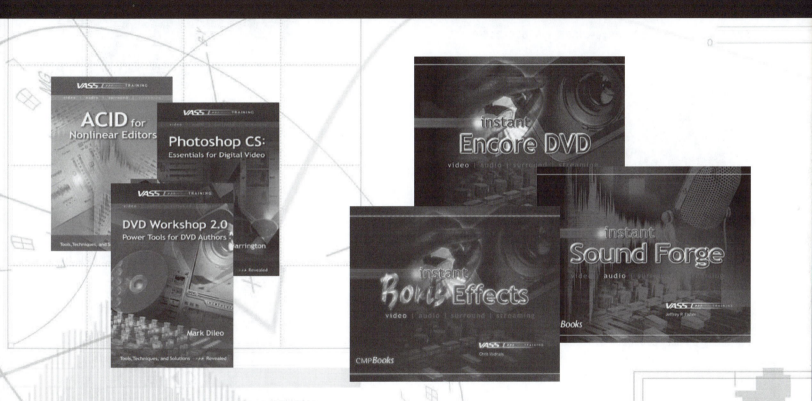

VASST Training Tours: visit vasst.com for current tour dates. We offer seminars on Cameras, Lighting, Editing, Surround Sound, and other general media topics. Training on specific applications by companies such as Adobe, Sony, Ulead, Pinnacle, AVID, Boris, and Apple is also available.

INSTANT SURROUND SOUND
JEFFREY P. FISHER

Unravel the mysteries of multi-channel audio processing for musical and visual environments. This comprehensive resource teaches techniques for mixing, and encoding for surround sound. It is packed with tips and tricks that help the reader to avoid the most common (and uncommon) pitfalls.

$24.95, Softcover, 191 pages, ISBN 1-57820-246-9

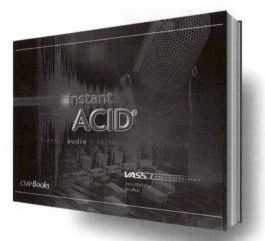

INSTANT ACID
JOHN ROFRANO & IACOBUS

Learn everything you need to know about Sony ACID software in an instant. This complete guide, designed as both a tutorial and quick reference, covers recording, adding effects, mixing and burning the final project, as well as interfacing with nonlinear video editing systems. The authors include personal tips and workflow habits to help you become productive quickly.

$24.95, Softcover, 242 pages, ISBN 1-57820-266-3

INSTANT SOUND FORGE
JEFFERY P. FISHER

Put this graphical cookbook of techniques to work in producing great audio with Sound Forge. Beginning with a review of the fundamental concepts, you get a complete guide to the audio production and post-production process with specific recipes for the most common challenges.

$24.95, Softcover, 209 pages, ISBN 1-57820-244-2

MAKE YOUR OWN MUSIC VIDEO
ED GASKELL

Make Your Own Music Video reveals the entire process in a single volume—for any ambitious moviemaker, musician or budding band manager who wants to take a crack at creating that breakthrough promo video, the one that may just end up on MTV. A music video pro tells all—from rehearsing the band and dealing with the egos, to the nitty-gritty of synching edited video and audio tracks and compressing footage for streaming on the Internet.

$44.95, 4-color softcover, 192 pages, ISBN 1-57820-258-2

DESIGNING DVD MENUS
MICHAEL BURNS & GEORGE CAIRNS

Design DVD menus with that cool, professional edge. Begin by cutting through the jargon and technical issues; then analyze an array of projects to see how to use animation, picture-within-picture, background movie clips, and audio and imaging effects to create stunning titles, menu screens, transitions, and interactive features.

$44.95, 4-color softcover, 192 pages, ISBN 1-57820-259-0

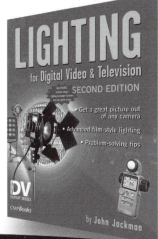

LIGHTING FOR DIGITAL VIDEO & TELEVISON, 2ND EDITION
JOHN JACKMAN

Get a complete course in video and television lighting from a seasoned pro. Detailed illustrations and real-world examples demonstrate proper equipment use, safety issues, troubleshooting, and staging techniques. This new edition features an 8-page full-color insert and new chapters on interview setups, as well as low-budget lighting set-ups on location.

$39.95, Softcover, 256 pages, ISBN 1-57820-251-5

CMP Books

www.cmpbooks.com